OFF-BEAT WALKS IN LONDON

A 'Discovering' guide

John Wittich and Ron Phillips

Shire Publications Ltd

CONTENTS

Walk 1   Around London Wall   **5**
St. Paul's Underground Station — St. Martin Le Grand
— Aldersgate — Gresham Street — Noble Street —
London Wall — Wood Street — Cheapside.

Walk 2   Lincoln's Inn Fields   **9**
Royal Courts of Justice, The Strand — Aldwych —
Houghton Street — Portugal Street — Portsmouth
Street — Lincoln's Inn — Serle Street — Carey Street
— Bell Yard — Temple Bar.

Walk 3   Thomas More's Chelsea   **17**
Chelsea Town Hall, King's Road — Glebe Place —
Upper Cheyne Row — Cheyne Row — Lordship
Place — Lawrence Street — Justice Walk — Old
Church Street — Margaret Roper Gardens — Danvers
Street — Battersea Bridge — Beaufort Street — King's
Road — Paultons Square.

Walk 4   Fleet Street and its tributaries   **21**
Temple Bar — Prince Henry's Room — St. Dunstan's-
in-the-West — Johnson Court — Gough Square —
Fleet Street — Cheshire Cheese — Salisbury Square
— St. Bride's Church — Ludgate Circus.

Walk 5   Precincts of Westminster Abbey   **27**
St. James's Park Underground Station — Queen Anne's
Gate — Dartmouth Street — Tothill Street — Broad
Sanctuary — St. Margaret's Church — Old Palace
Yard — Millbank — Dean Stanley Street — Smith
Square — Lord North Street — Cowley Street —
Barton Street — Great College Street — Dean's Yard
— Westminster Abbey.

Walk 6   In the steps of the Blackfriars   **33**
Blackfriars Underground Station — Mermaid Theatre
— Upper Thames Street — St. Benet's Hill — Queen
Victoria Street — Godliman Street — Knightrider
Street — Carter Lane — Dean's Court — Wardrobe
Place — St. Andrew's Hill — Ireland Yard — Play-
house Yard — Church Entry — Carter Lane —
Blackfriars Lane — The Black Friar public house.

Walk 7 **Mayfair—on the course of the Tyburn**   **40**
Green Park Underground Station — Piccadilly —
Whitehorse Street — Shepherd Market — Curzon
Street — Queen Street, Mayfair — Charles Street —
Berkeley Square — Hill Street — Farm Street — South
Audley Street — Grosvenor Square.

Walk 8 **Great Fire of London**   **47**
The Monument — Monument Street — St. Mary at
Hill — Eastcheap — Philpot Lane — Lime Street —
Leadenhall Market — Leadenhall Street — Cornhill
— St. Peter's Church — St. Michael's Church — St.
Michael's Alley — Castle Court — Ball Court —
Birchin Lane — Change Alley — Lombard Street
— King William Street — The Monument.

Index   **54**

*Copyright © 1969, 1973 and 1977 by John Wittich and Ron Phillips. No.
63 in the 'Discovering' series. ISBN 0 85263 378 5. First published 1969;
reprinted 1970. Second edition 1973. This third edition published 1977. All
rights reserved. No part of this publication may be reproduced or
transmitted in any form or by any means, electronic or mechanical,
including photocopy, recording, or any information storage and retrieval
system, without permission in writing from the publishers, Shire
Publications Ltd., Cromwell House, Church Street, Princes Risborough,
Aylesbury, Bucks, HP17 9AJ, U.K.*

Printed in Great Britain by C. I. Thomas & Sons (Haverfordwest) Ltd,
Press Buildings, Merlins Bridge, Haverfordwest.

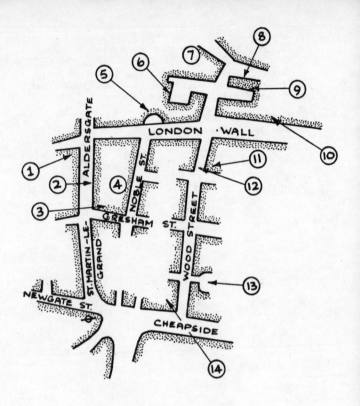

Walk 1. Around London Wall

1. St. Botolph's, Aldersgate
2. Aldersgate plaque
3. St. Anne and St. Agnes
4. Roman city wall
5. Roman barracks
6. Barber Surgeon's Hall
7. St. Giles', Cripplegate
8. Bomb plaque
9. Roman city wall
10. Elsing Priory
11. Police station
12. St. Alban's tower
13. Wood Street compter
14. St. Peter's railings

St. Paul's Underground Station — St. Martin Le Grand — Aldersgate — Gresham Street — Noble Street — London Wall — Wood Street — Cheapside.

To walk the entire length of the old city wall one would have to tramp over three miles, starting at the Tower of London and, by following a roughly half-circular course, ending up at Blackfriars before covering the length of Upper and Lower Thames Streets. However, for the purpose of this walk we have chosen an area in which several portions of the wall can still be clearly seen.

It was late in the second century A.D. that a wall was first constructed of stone around the then perimeter of the City of London. When completed it enclosed some 330 acres of land, making it the fifth largest city in the Roman Empire.

As London had no stone quarries of its own the stone was 'imported' from Kent, being called, in fact, Kentish Ragstone. The outside faces of the wall were made up of stones which had been 'squared-off' and so presented a fairly smooth surface. In between the facings was poured concrete and other stones to make up the hard centre. In front was a ditch; behind, on the city side, an earthen ramp was built as an added protection against any enemy trying to burrow through. The wall's height was from 30 to 35 feet, and along the inner side there was a sentry walk along which soldiers guarding the city would keep watch.

Our walk starts from **St. Paul's Underground Station** from where St. Martin Le Grand meets with Newgate Street and Cheapside.

The name St. Martin Le Grand reminds one that here, in the Middle Ages, was one of London's many monasteries. The bell in the church tower here would ring out every evening to tell the citizens of London to 'cover their fires, shut up their shutters and go to bed'. This was the curfew, rung from several of the church towers throughout medieval times. Like so many other monasteries, St. Martin Le Grand was dissolved in the sixteenth century and its stone used for other purposes; much of it went to help build the first Somerset House in the Strand.

Walking up **St. Martin Le Grand,** passing, on the left-hand side of the road, some of the numerous offices of the Post Office Headquarters, one comes to the church of **St. Botolph's, Aldersgate (1),** one of the three remaining London churches dedicated to this Saxon saint from Boston, Lincolnshire. As with the others, this church is just outside the place where the city gate once stood, which is not at all surprising as Botolph is a patron saint of the huntsmen who would have travelled through the gates of the city to hunt in the forests of Middlesex and Essex. The present church dates from the eighteenth century and is one of the few churches not to have been rebuilt by Sir Christopher Wren after the Great Fire of London of 1666. In the churchyard, known familiarly as the Postmen's Park, can be found the **Geo. Fred. Watts Memorial Cloisters.** In these cloisters are commemorated many deeds of heroism by everyday people who lost their lives trying to save others. One plaque, for instance, tells the story of a young girl in Union Street in the Borough who, having saved three children from a fire, died while trying to rescue a fourth child.

Retracing one's steps a few yards, on a building almost opposite the church is a 'blue plaque' **(2)** placed by the City Corporation to mark the spot where Aldersgate once stood.

The origin of the name **Aldersgate** is either because it was one of the older gates of the city (it was the north gate of the Roman city when there were only four gates in the city wall), or because the building, or rebuilding, of the gate was sponsored by someone whose name was Ealdred. There is mention of it by name in a document of 1289, which would make it concerned with an order of the same century which read 'All gates of the City are to be open by day, and at each gate there are to be two sergeants to open the same, skilful men, and fluent of speech, who are to keep watch on persons coming and going so that no evil shall befall the City'. A similar order of the fourteenth century commanded that 'all gates are to be closed every night on the hour of the Curfew being rung'. Also, regulations were made that gates should be guarded by 12 men by day and 24 by night who were to be 'able-bodied, well instructed and well armed'. Originally, in the Middle Ages, every able-bodied man in the city was made to 'stand guard at the gates', but later the wealthier merchants paid others to do their tour of duty. When the gate was rebuilt in the early part of the seventeenth century it was quite a handsome building, three storeys high, with flanking towers. On the outer face was a statue of James I of England in his Chair of State, recalling that as James VI of Scotland he passed through this gateway on his acceptance of the throne of England. The gate was finally demolished in the eighteenth century, but not before a printer by the name of John Day had used it as his printing works.

Moving down on the left-hand side of the road, towards St. Paul's Station, one comes to **Gresham Street,** which reminds us of one of the great names in the history of the city—Sir Thomas Gresham, founder of the Royal Exchange and Gresham College.

6

Just inside Gresham Street is the church of **St. Anne and St. Agnes (3).** Severely damaged in the last war, it was carefully rebuilt to the original designs of Sir Christopher Wren and is now used by a Latvian congregation. Note the large 'A' on the church tower's weathervane. Once this church was described as 'St. Anne's-in-the-willows', a pleasant reminder of a nearby stream that has long since disappeared. Look for the tasteful junction box in the churchyard.

A few yards from the church is **Noble Street,** named after Thos. Le Noble who lived here in the fourteenth century. Walk up the street and you will find extensive remains of the **Roman city wall (4).** Notice particularly the portion nearest to the church where you can see the city wall joined with that of a fort which was built before the wall itself. Notice too the little culvert built into the lower portion allowing a small stream to pass through without undermining the strength of the wall. Follow the line of the wall and you will find several stretches of it running parallel to Noble Street. You will then come to the broad modern roadway called London Wall. This is a post-war thoroughfare built to allow modern transport to move more freely where once the Roman chariots were housed.

Crossing **London Wall** one sees the Museum of London to the left. But before taking to the upper pedestrian ways seek out the entrance to the old fort of London, now nestling by the side of an underground car park. Choose your time well and you will be able to descend to the level of the Roman city and see the foundations of the old guardhouse of London's first fortified barracks **(5).** The times of opening are Mondays to Fridays, from 12.30 p.m. to 2 p.m. only. Leaving the fort find the nearest stairway which will take you to the upper pedestrian walks and you will find yourself in twenty-first century London. Look down into the square behind at the new **Barber Surgeon's Hall (6),** built right into the city wall itself. It is hard to think today of this city company being responsible not only for haircuts and shaving but also for blood-letting, the 'cure' for so many ills of previous ages. This is why barbers had poles outside their establishments painted red, white and blue; white for the shaving and haircuts, red for the blood and blue for the veins; signs which have now almost disappeared from the streets of London. Over the top of the flats one can see the tower of **St. Giles' Cripplegate (7),** one of the largest parish churches in the city. Find another staircase nearby, descend to ground level once more and pay a visit to the church. We pass on the way another 'blue plaque' which shows us where Cripplegate once stood, but we will return there later.

St. Giles is another patron saint of huntsmen, and again,

appropriately, is found just outside the city wall on the road to the forests. The church was rebuilt after a fire in the middle of the sixteenth century, escaped damage in the Great Fire of 1666, only to be completely gutted in the bombing of 1940. Here Oliver Cromwell was married to Elizabeth Bourchier; here Milton was buried, in the church which earlier saw him re-united to his first wife, Mary Powell. In the churchyard is one of the bastions of the city wall.

Retracing our steps we come to **Fore Street,** and on the side of Roman House is a plaque **(8)** which tells us that here fell the city's first explosive bomb in the Second World War. Peep inside the foyer of Roman House and you will see on the wall in the entrance doorway a mural depicting London in the time of the Romans. Returning to the upper pedestrian way, we find the **Cripplegate** plaque, already mentioned. Like Aldersgate this too has alternative origins for its name, but it most probably derives from the Anglo-Saxon word *crepel* which means den or underground passage. There was an underground entrance to the city here in the Middle Ages. Once the gates of the city were closed after the curfew had ceased to ring there was only one place you could legally enter and that was here at Cripplegate. You had to prove your identity in some way and, provided the guards were satisfied that you belonged to the city, and had, as you maintained, only been seeing your girl friend home, being late back because of a tiff, you were then let back in. Like others this gate too was maintained as a prison at one time; also it is on record as having been used as a dwelling house for the Common Cryer of the City of London. At one time the gate was rebuilt at the expense of the Worshipful Company of Brewers, which doubtless suited their purposes very well, as it led to the fields outside the city wall where the apprentices and others practiced the noble art—and thirsty work—of warfare. Like Aldersgate, Cripplegate was demolished in the eighteenth century and sold for ninety pounds.

Now turn left by the side of Roman House, and you will come to one of the most magnificent stretches of London's **city wall (9)** still clearly visible. Carefully descend the stairway to the side of the wall and you will be able to imagine quite easily how formidable a cliff the wall would have presented anybody wishing to enter illegally. Retrace your steps to the roadway and another set of stairs which lead to the upper walks once more. Look back now, downwards to the wall, tiny against the great modern buildings towering over it. One wonders which will last longer! Almost immediately behind you now stand the remains of yet another monastic establishment, the former **Elsing Priory (10),** founded in the fourteenth century by Sir William de Elsing as a

8

hospital for one hundred blind men who were turned out at the time of the Dissolution of the Monasteries. It then became a private dwelling until a fire in the latter half of the sixteenth century destroyed most of it, except the chapel which was used by the nearby parish of St. Alphage as its church. It was finally demolished in 1924 leaving this rare example of medieval architecture to be later surrounded by modern office blocks.

While remaining in the upper walks cross the bridge over London Wall and descend on the other side into **Wood Street,** probably once the resort of woodworkers. Today, however, it contains the new **City of London police station (11),** which has as its front door neighbour the tower of **St. Alban's (12),** all that remains of a church rebuilt in the seventeenth century by Inigo Jones, and later repaired by Sir Christopher Wren after the Great Fire of London.

Continuing down Wood Street one finds on the left-hand side an entrance marked Mitre Court, the end of which opens into a courtyard. In the centre stands the entrance to the old **Wood Street Compter (13)** (prison), now used as a store for wine, etc.

Returning once more to Wood Street turn left and you will soon find yourself by some iron railings marking the site of the church of **St. Peter's West Chepe (14).** The church itself was not rebuilt after the Great Fire but the symbol of St. Peter—the crossed keys—can still be seen entwined in the railings. A few yards further on and you are in Cheapside, a hundred yards from where you started this walk.

Walk 2   Lincoln's Inn Fields

Royal Courts of Justice, The Strand — Aldwych — Houghton Street — Portugal Street — Portsmouth Street — Lincoln's Inn — Serle Street — Carey Street — Bell Yard — Temple Bar.

Although this walk is directed to the highly interesting off-beat precinct adjacent to Lincoln's Inn, we shall also be wandering in and out of streets which were once part of Central London's worst slum. Consisting of some 28 acres, containing, for example, Wych Street, Holywell Street and Clare Market, this area was notorious for its gin-houses, brothels and thieves' kitchens. So old and mouldering were the buildings in these shambles that often, during the 1900–1905 clearances, houses deprived of their neighbours collapsed of their own accord. Many of the nineteenth century alleys still remain as 'rights of way' and a walker with an imaginative eye might be able to catch for a moment the horrors of the 'good old days'.

As the walk commences at the **Law Courts (1)**, or the Royal Courts of Justice—to give them their official title—perhaps the best vantage point would be the island in the centre of the roadway. At a first viewing the building gives the impression of being a very old baronial castle—Scottish perhaps—complete with spires and turrets. However, one would be greatly mistaken, since the complex dates from 1874–80, before which time the Royal Courts of Justice were based at the Palace of Westminster.

Designed by George Edmund Street, a pupil of Sir Gilbert Scott, the Courts architecturally represent 'the last fling of the Gothic Revival', a period which gave London the Houses of Parliament, St. Pancras Station and a host of similar structures. The styling was extremely romantic, with pleasant arcading, a minimum of symmetrical layout and no mean distribution of statuary. The site is one of eight acres with a perimeter of about half-a-mile, and prior to the preparation for its present purpose was covered by 33 streets and bye-ways of the Wych Street rookery containing 300–400 houses and 4,000 people.

The interior includes 30 courthouses of various sizes, all serving the Supreme Court of Judicature for England and Wales. Cases heard here cover three divisions of law, namely: Chancery, Queen's Bench, and Probate, Divorce and Admiralty, these last three always being grouped together. Criminal cases, except for appeals, are heard elsewhere, principally at the Central Criminal Court, more popularly known as the Old Bailey.

Look up over the entrance gateway and one can see three statues. The central one is of Christ with His hand raised in blessing, the supreme lawmaker; on the left can be seen King Solomon, and on the right is King Alfred. (The outside rear of the building in Casey Street has a statue of Moses and the Ten Commandments.)

Towards the end of October the annual ceremony of Paying the Quit Rents takes place at the Law Courts. The public are admitted to watch these colourful proceedings during which payment of rent for two portions of land is handed over to the Queen's Remembrancer by the City of London. This really is in every way an off-beat occasion, for the whereabouts of both pieces of real estate are virtually unknown, although one is called the 'Moors', in the county of Shropshire and the other is the 'Forge' at St. Clement Danes. For the first a rent of two faggots cut with a billhook is accepted, and for the other the Crown receives six horse-shoes and 61 nails! The same shoes and nails have been changing hands for 500 years!

Still on the central island in the roadway, before starting the walk, note the bollards at the curbside, designed to match the nearby Gothic pile and, above all, a most magnificent lamp post,

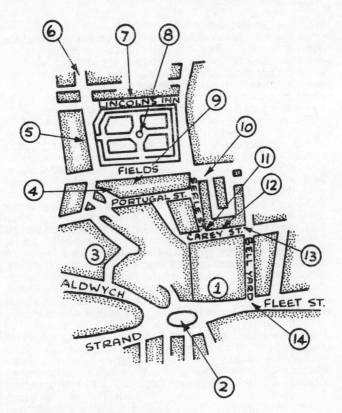

Walk 2. Lincoln's Inn Fields

1. Law Courts
2. St. Clement Danes
3. London School of Economics
4. Old Curiosity Shop
5. Conyingham's house
6. The Ship tavern
7. Soane's Museum
8. Execution site
9. Royal College of Surgeons
10. Lincoln's Inn gateway
11. Statue of Thomas More
12. Boundary stones
13. Six-bay house of 1731
14. Temple Bar

picked out in gold and bearing a veritable candelabra of lights.

On the same island one finds the very realistic figure of Dr. Samuel Johnson (warts and all) facing Fleet Street and the quarter of the city in which he became a legend. He holds in his hand the first dictionary of the English language which he had compiled. Nearby a plaque shows us the site of the Holywell which gave its name to a nearby street as well as to some not so holy water percolating up through the graveyard.

We can now examine the church of **St. Clement Danes (2).** It is dedicated to the saint who was martyred by being bound to an anchor and cast overboard. The latter part of the church's name springs from the time when, after the Danes had been driven out of England, those who had married Englishwomen and remained here, were ordered to live in this district. It is thought by some that Harold I, a Dane by birth, was buried here. Most Londoners feel a close affinity to St. Clements because of the familiar nursery rhyme *Oranges and Lemons*, the tune of which has long been rung on the bells. Although the pre-Great Fire St. Clements escaped the fate of so many London churches during that catastrophe, by 1680 it was unsafe enough to merit re-building and Christopher Wren, then at the peak of his creativity, produced a structure of rare beauty. James Gibbs completed the church by adding the steeple in the eighteenth century. During the night of 10th May 1941, the church was reduced to a shell; the famous bells, except for the Sanctus, were destroyed too.

In 1955 work was started on restoration, Wren's original design being kept in mind, and now we have a superb 'Wren reproduction'. The church was re-dedicated and now serves as a memorial to the Royal Air Force; £150,000 was raised from the Commonwealth and other allied nations to cherish the memory of those who had defended our freedom. The Royal Family was present for the re-dedication in October 1958 as were representatives of the air forces of the Commonwealth. The floor of the church contains over 700 slate carvings of badges of the squadrons and units of the R.A.F. and there are 800 hassocks, all of different embroidery designs, that were made and presented by men and women all over the world. Three windows in contemporary stained glass dominate the altar end of the church. But above all it is the glorious interior, in silver grey and white, and the golden dome of the apse that draws the eye.

The famous bells, what was left of them, were taken back to the Whitechapel Bell Foundry where they had been manufactured in 1693. They were recast and today ring out the nursery rhyme at 9 a.m., 12 noon, 3 p.m. and 6 p.m., just as they have done for nearly three centuries. The carillon also includes *The Old Hundredth* and the *Royal Air Force March* in its repertoire.

Crossing from the island towards Australia House we turn right, crossing over the road which is one of London's finest crescents—**Aldwych.** Created at the turn of the century by the clearance of the Wych Street slums, Aldwych has many fine commercial buildings and is dominated at the central portion by the great complex of Bush House, named after Irving T. Bush, an American businessman. The main entrance facing the wide vista of Kingsway is topped by two very large statues representing the friendship of the English-speaking peoples. One of these suffered damage during the war but was not repaired because the 'war-wounds', so it was thought, drew the alliance closer.

A few yards further on we enter Houghton Street and the 'revolutionary' precinct of the **London School of Economics (3).** Part of London University, L.S.E. has produced many of the father figures of the Labour Party; it continues in this tradition with its students always in the vanguard of protest on every issue of political importance.

Continue left into Clare Market, once heart of the great slums, prior to the clearances. The name stems from the Earl of Clare who in 1617 was granted the right to set up a market around which the mean streets grew, as did the poor and miserable local population.

We go next to the **Old Curiosity Shop (4),** having turned right from Clare Market into Portugal Street and then left into Portsmouth Street. At the end we see the tiny antique shop that has long been famous as one of London's main tourist attractions. There are those who would quarrel with the claim that Charles Dickens used this as his model. But there can be no doubt that he knew the little shop very well since he often gave readings from his novels at a nearby house. Whether the visitor is sceptical or not, the 'home of little Nell and her grandfather' is certainly worth a quick look round.

Now leaving the shop on our right, we cross **Sardinia Street** to the west side of Lincoln's Inn Fields. The street name is a memory of the Catholic chapel of the Sardinian Embassy, sited here, which twice served as a target for anti-popery rioters. Dickens refers to the final outbreak of 1760 in his book *Barnaby Rudge.*

Lincoln's Inn Fields were first built upon in 1618 on this west side, and battle commenced between those who sought to profit by building houses, and the Society of Lincoln's Inn, whose members owned the land. During this period Inigo Jones, the famous architect, was commissioned to lay out the central portion as a garden. Two hundred and fifty years later Lincoln's Inn Fields were purchased by the London County Council and thrown open to the public.

Before entering the gardens, we should continue along the west side. **Nos. 57 and 58** were originally a 1640 house remodelled by the great Leoni in 1730 and divided into two a few years later. The latter house was lived in by John Forster, Dickens's biographer, and it was here that the readings referred to earlier took place. Dickens mentions the house in one of his stories, as the home of Mr Tulkinghorn, a character in *Bleak House*.

Nos. 59 and 60 (5), attributed to Inigo Jones and built for Sir David Conyingham in 1640, were also eventually split into a pair of houses. **Newcastle House** is on the corner at No. 66 and, as the plaque at the top indicates, is by Sir Edward Lutyens who copied this building from a previous one by John Vanbrugh, builder of Blenheim Palace for the Duke of Marlborough. At the side, in Remnant Street, the pleasant arcading over the pavement is all that is left of Vanbrugh's original work.

Continue for a moment into Gate Street and at the end we find a tavern of great historic interest—**The Ship (6).** Here, during the Catholic persecution, religious services were held thanks to a sympathetic proprietor. Worshippers would enter the bars as ordinary customers, call for ale and pass into the parlour. If, however, suspected government spies were around the congregation would get a discreet wink from the potman and hold their ales until the danger was over. The service, of course, would be temporarily abandoned, with the priest hidden away somewhere upstairs.

Retracing our steps we turn left along the north side of the Fields to No. 13. This is the **Sir John Soane's Museum (7),** an incredible collection of antiquities left *in situ* by the famous Georgian architect. Here, amongst other delights, one can find the alabaster sarcophagus of Pharaoh Seti I, father of Rameses the Great, a death mask of Sarah Siddons, and an astounding picture gallery notable for the two series of paintings by William Hogarth: *The Rake's Progress* and *The Election.*

Cross the road now and enter the central path into the gardens. At the centre, under the roof of a shelter, can be found a brass plaque marking an execution site **(8).** This is where, in 1683, Lord William Russell was beheaded for his complicity in the Rye House plot, and where, about a hundred years before, Anthony Babington and 14 others were hanged, drawn and quartered for trying to procure the escape of Mary, Queen of Scots, after her imprisonment by Elizabeth I. Walk through to the other side of the gardens and, before turning left, look at the fine building by Sir Charles Barry constructed in 1835 for the **Royal College of Surgeons (9),** with a portico by George Dance.

Ahead now can be seen the gateway into **Lincoln's Inn (10),** one of the four Inns of Court. These serve as chambers for those practising at the Bar and here aspiring barristers 'keep terms' by dining in hall on a specific number of occasions during their period of training.

The Inn derives its name from Henry de Lacey, Earl of Lincoln (d. 1311), who turned his town house over to law students and legal practitioners. The oldest building in the vast complex is the 1491 **Old Hall,** which was extended in 1624 by Inigo Jones and restored in 1928. It contains a large religious painting by Hogarth. The enormous **New Hall** of 1843 is by Philip Hardwick, styled in neo-Tudor and bearing both the date and initials of the architect in brick diapering. The library next door is thought to have the oldest and most comprehensive collection of law books in the world. Although one is allowed to walk, by privilege and not by right, around the precincts, the Chapel is the only building open to the public. It is well worth a visit since it is the work of Inigo Jones and was finished in 1623; it is unusual in that the Chapel is raised over a ground-level crypt. Strolling about the pleasant seventeenth and eighteenth century squares and buildings of Lincoln's Inn is a delightful way of passing time.

Leave again by the gate and turn left into Serle Street and left again into Carey Street noting the statue of **Sir Thomas More (11)** over a doorway on the corner. The name of this street is associated with empty pockets, for until some years ago the Bankruptcy Court was one of its buildings, but there is still much of interest. Within yards of the corner we find the **Seven Stars** pub, a reminder of the days when the Dutch, engaged in welding the seven Netherlands provinces into a nation, sometimes took refuge in England. Next, a little further on, look for the two oldest **parish boundary stones (12)** in central London. They are at the bottom of a wall at pavement level; one marks the parish of St. Clement Danes by means of an anchor; the other bears the letters S.D.W.—St. Dunstan's in the West. Finally, before turning right into Bell Yard, there is a fine **six-bay house of 1731 (13),** perfectly symmetrical—except for its drainpipe!

Bell Yard, entered now, is named after a long-since vanished tavern. Samuel Pepys, the diarist, refers to his first dabble at gambling in a house here; Charles Dickens in 1831 used No. 5 during his early days as a reporter and, as might be expected, later used the Yard for a scene in *Bleak House*.

At the end of Bell Yard we have reached **Temple Bar (14),** only a stone's throw from where we started.

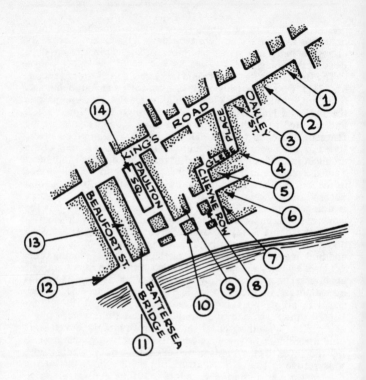

Walk 3. Thomas More's Chelsea

1. Old Town Hall
2. Six Bells
3. Argyll House
4. Hunting Lodge
5. Upper Cheyne Row
6. Church
7. Carlyle's house
8. Monmouth House
9. Smollet/Fielding plaque
10. All Saints
11. Crosby Hall
12. Lindsay House
13. Site of Thomas More's house
14. Paultons Square

Chelsea Town Hall, King's Road — Glebe Place — Upper Cheyne Row — Cheyne Row — Lordship Place — Lawrence Street — Justice Walk — Old Church Street — Margaret Roper Gardens — Danvers Street — Battersea Bridge — Beaufort Street — King's Road — Paultons Square.

Thomas More, or to give him his full title, Saint Sir Thomas More, was born in Milk Street, off Cheapside, in 1478. His father was a judge and it was natural that young Thomas should follow in his father's footsteps as he did when he became a law student at Lincoln's Inn. In 1501 he was called to the Bar, and three years later entered Parliament beginning a highly successful career which culminated in his acceptance of the Lord Chancellorship in 1529. Meanwhile, he had married Jane Colt, by whom he had three daughters and one son, but Jane died young and More then married the widow Alice Middleton. As a judge he was incorruptible, as Henry VIII soon found out when he tried to persuade More that his marriage to Catherine of Aragon was invalid; More resigned the Chancellorship and retired from public life to his house in Chelsea; he was later tried, found guilty of treason, and executed at Tower Hill on the 6th July, 1535. His last words to the spectators around the scaffold were 'I am the King's good servant, but God's first'.

During the past few years the King's Road, Chelsea, once a private road used only by the king on his way to Hampton Court, has become noted for its fashions and for being part of the so-called Swinging London scene. Our walk starts at the former **Town Hall (1)** of the Borough of Chelsea—now merged with the Royal Borough of Kensington to form the Royal Borough of Kensington and Chelsea. The Town Hall was the work of the architect J. M. Brydon and dates from 1886, with extensions at the turn of this century. We turn left and walk down the road to one of the largest public houses in London, the **Six Bells (2)**. Recently remodelled, it now serves as a public house throughout the week, but in addition houses a discotheque.

Crossing Oakley Street one finds, still in the King's Road, a group of early eighteenth century houses which offer the visitor some idea of the type of small town house that once adorned many parts of the metropolis. **Argyll House (3)**, designed by Leoni in 1723, is No. 211 King's Road and No. 215 was the home at one time of Dr Thomas Arne who wrote, among other items, *Rule Britannia*. In this group can be seen a plaque stating that Ellen Terry the famous actress lived here in the 1920s.

We now reach **Glebe Place** and, turning down it, leave the hustle of the King's Road behind us, pausing occasionally to note the different styles of the houses, including many with large studio windows facing north. Just as the street turns sharply to the right note the charming little cottage **(4)** on your left, a gentle reminder that Chelsea was once a little village far out in the wilds of Middlesex. The Place turns, and turns again, until one finds oneself on the corner of **Upper Cheyne Row.** Here it is worth turning left to admire the houses **(5)**, again noting that at one of them, No. 22, Leigh Hunt lived between the years 1833 and 1840, while No. 28 proudly displays the date 1767. This whole range is typical of the smaller, cheaper houses built behind the larger ones that once spread along the entire river front by Chelsea Reach.

The church (6) on the corner of Upper Cheyne Row and Cheyne Row, designed by Goldie and opened in 1895, is on the site of the famous De Morgan Pottery Works. Anyone interested in De Morgan Pottery should visit Old Battersea House across the river in Battersea. Architecturally the Row presents a similar rhythm to that of Queen Anne's Gate near St. James's Park Station, dating as it does from c. 1708. Like so many streets in Chelsea the Row claims several famous inhabitants, among them Thomas Carlyle, who lived for nearly 50 years at **No. 24 (7).** His house, now the property of the National Trust, is regularly open to members of the public from Tuesdays to Sundays throughout the year. Among the many treasures shown to visitors is the double-walled room in the attic which kept out the noises of the town while he was working on one of his many books.

A short distance from Carlyle's house one comes to **Lawrence Street,** via Lordship Place, and although Lawrence House has long since been demolished the name, from a sub-Lord of the Manor, remains. In this street, like Cheyne Row, many famous persons have lived. Note Duke's House and Monmouth House on the way **(8)**, and find the 'blue plaque' **(9)** further along commemorating Tobias Smollet and Henry Fielding, who with John Gay, composer of the *Beggars' Opera*, have helped bring fame and fortune to the street. This is a road of contrasts: compare the Georgian cottages opposite Duke's and Monmouth Houses, with the mid-Victorian Peabody Estate Buildings on the opposite side of the road.

Return down the street and, facing Duke's House, you will find **Justice Walk.** Half way along is the old court house with the barred gates of the cells underneath. This short walk leads into **Old Church Street;** turn left, and you come to All Saints, the old parish church of Chelsea.

Much of **All Saints (10)** was destroyed during the last war and had to be rebuilt. However, thanks to the excellent work of the late Walter Godfrey, only the really experienced eye will be able to detect the restored from the rebuilt. It was in 1528 that Thomas More built the south chapel of the church, one of the earliest works of the Renaissance in the London area. It has a distinctly French atmosphere and is said to be the work of Holbein. Among the monuments in the chapel is one to Thomas More, with the inscription composed by More himself. Tradition has it that his headless body was buried in this chapel. In one corner of the churchyard note the tomb of Sir Hans Sloane, who, besides leaving his name to several streets in Chelsea, gave us the Chelsea Physic Garden, the basic collection of what is now the British Museum, and a number of books on botanical subjects. The tomb's urn is made of Coade stone, an artificial stone made in a factory on the South Bank where the Royal Festival Hall now stands. In 1969 a seated statue of Thomas More was unveiled in front of the church. It is the work of L. Cubitt Bevis and shows him, with the chain of the chancellor on his lap, looking towards the spot from which he took his leave of his family. Inscribed on the front of the statue is a copy of his signature.

Walking in the direction of the bridge seen from the west doorway of the church one first comes to the **Margaret Roper Gardens**, commemorating More's daughter who married into the Roper family, and in whose family vault at Canterbury the head of Thomas More was buried.

Danvers Street further on recalls Sir John Danvers, one of the signatories of the death warrant of Charles I. The gardens at Danvers House were laid out in the early part of the seventeenth century, but disappeared by the end of it.

On the corner of Danvers Street and the Chelsea Embankment, the latter completed in 1871, stands the former hall of Sir John Crosby. **Crosby Hall (11)**, built in 1466, once stood in Bishopsgate in the city, but due to road widening schemes and rebuilding at the turn of the century, was scheduled for demolition. It was saved, dismantled stone by stone and beam by beam, and brought here where it now forms part of a hall of residence for university women. It is open to the public daily, including Sundays. Incidentally, Thomas More lived for a time in Crosby Hall when it was in the city.

Battersea Bridge lies almost opposite the Hall and the present bridge, dating from 1890, replaces the old timber one immortalised in paintings by Turner, Whistler and Greaves. A number of the latter artist's works are in the London Museum showing Chelsea and its associations with the river in earlier days.

Looking upstream from the foot of the bridge one's eyes are

arrested by the silhouette of **Lots Road Power Station,** not one of the most glamorous buildings in London, but certainly one of the most useful as it supplies much of the power needed to drive London Transport's complicated network of underground railways. It derives its name from the Common Lots or Lammas Lands where, from August to February, cattle were allowed to graze. Later the area became the famous Cremorne Pleasure Gardens.

Opposite the foot of the bridge is Cheyne Walk and by turning to the left, away from the side of the church, one finds another interesting group of eighteenth century houses. Here too is the only remaining large-scale riverside house, **Lindsay House (12)** dating from circa 1674. It was originally a three-storeyed house but about a hundred years later it was sub-divided into its present form. Count Zinzendorf lived here for a time when it became the headquarters of the Moravians in England. Here too lived Whistler as well as Sir Marc Brunel, builder of the Thames Tunnel, and his more famous son Isambard Kingdom Brunel, the engineer of the Great Western Railway.

But we must retrace our steps from the foot of the bridge and turn left up into **Beaufort Street,** walking up the very line of the avenue which led to Beaufort House where Thomas More lived until that fatal day in 1534 when he was taken by boat to the Tower of London. Today the site **(13)** is occupied by another building, and all that remains in the area of More's time is an old mulberry tree under which, it is said, he used to sit and meditate.

Continuing to walk up Beaufort Street one comes, once more, to the King's Road. Turn right and pass a number of interesting squares of which **Paultons Square (14)** rates a special note, being an excellent example of a town square of the 1830s with terraced houses built on a unified plan. In a few minutes you will find yourself back at Chelsea Town Hall.

Temple Bar — Prince Henry's Room — St. Dunstan's-in-the-West — Johnson Court — Gough Square — Fleet Street — Cheshire Cheese — Salisbury Square — St. Bride's Church — Ludgate Circus.

Think of Fleet Street and you think of newsprint. Think of Fleet Street and you think of Dr Johnson. Yet the street has more to offer than journalism and gossip. Few people may know of the noble houses belonging to the bishops and abbots which, before the Reformation, once lined the street between the city and Westminster. Even fewer realise that the name springs from a hidden river flowing down from London's northern heights to enter the Thames near Blackfriars Bridge—the river Fleet.

Fleet Street begins and ends at its western frontier at **Temple Bar (1)** where this walk commences. Here are the first, and the last, buildings—if we are to believe street numbering. Once the western gates of the city were at Newgate and Ludgate, but some time before 1293, London stretched itself out to Holborn and Temple Bars. No one knows exactly when; the date is only relevant to the first recorded mention of the expansion. Temple Bar was an office for the collection of tolls and duties and a barrier against rogues entering or leaving. Being on the direct route between the city and the Palace of Westminster, it was also the place where the sovereign paid (and still pays) due respect to the power and might of the citizens of London. Many will have seen old prints portraying Temple Bar and there is a bas-relief on the present day plinth that stands in the roadway. Wren built that gateway between 1670 and 1672. Apart from the traditional uses, it served, in its time, as an office for Child's Bank, the local lock-up, and a pin cushion for a set of gruesome spikes upon which well-known and freshly executed heads were placed. Temple Bar was demolished in 1878, after nearly 100 years of agitation for its removal, being re-erected sometime later on the estate of Sir Henry Meux at Theobalds Park in Hertfordshire where it remains to this day. The memorial now standing in its place—causing as much obstruction to traffic as did the Bar—bears on its top a dragon representing the City of London.

Child's Bank is No. 1 Fleet Street, within yards of the plinth, most unbanklike in appearance but with a long history. Founded by Sir Francis Child, the first goldsmith to become a banker, its customers have included Charles II, Nell Gwynne and Samuel Pepys whose accounts can now be examined in Glynn Mills Bank in Lombard Street. Charles Dickens transformed Child's into Tellson's in his *Tale of Two Cities*. The bank still retains a memory of its earlier days, before street numbering became the rule, for we can see outside 'The sign of the Marigold'.

Moving on now, a little to the right is a large classical front-age serving as the entrance to the **Middle Temple (2).** This gateway, often attributed to Wren, was in fact designed by Roger North, an amateur architect and a bencher, and bears on the keystone a lamb and flag, emblem of the Middle Temple, and '1684' the year of its construction. There is a little balcony and below are great studded doors. A peep through into Middle Temple Lane, which divides the Inner from the Middle Temple, reveals a scene straight out of the 1690s with a row of houses complete with overhanging upper floors.

Returning to Fleet Street, opposite Chancery Lane one sees another relic of old London—**Prince Henry's Room (3)**—with its Jacobean gabling and double overhang, a building of 1610 which may have been used as the office of the Duchy of Cornwall under Prince Henry, son of James I—hence the title. Serving once as a waxworks exhibition and later as a public house, today it is maintained by the City of London Corporation. Entrance is 10p and the room, with a magnificent ceiling and panelled walls, is well worth a visit. The archway below leads into the Inner Temple.

A few more steps and on the left-hand side of the roadway we arrive at **St. Dunstan's-in-the-West (4),** so called to prevent confusion with a church, dedicated to that saint, on the other side of the city. Looking at the top of St. Dunstan's for the first time one is struck by the tower's singularly beautiful architecture not unlike that of All Saints, Pavement, at York. St. Dunstan's was built in 1829–33 by John Shaw to replace another which had to go as a result of Fleet Street being widened. (It is hardly the widest of thoroughfares even now!) First mentioned in a document of 1185 the church is closely associated with two great preachers: William Tyndale, who first translated the New Testament into English and who was martyred in 1536, and John Donne the famous Dean of Old St. Paul's Cathedral. Isaak Walton, a parishioner and biographer of Donne, had his classic *The Compleat Angler* published from the churchyard and there is a window to his memory in the present octagonal church. Some of the statuary embellishing the 1586 Ludgate at the time of its demolition in 1760 was removed to St. Dunstan's, like the fine statue of Queen Elizabeth I now seen over the vestry porch. Perhaps the passer-by is more impressed with the bracket clock, one of London's best-known. Made in 1671, every 60 minutes it causes the two club-bearing figures to strike the bell. This clock was removed to a villa in Regents Park and only returned to Fleet Street in 1936.

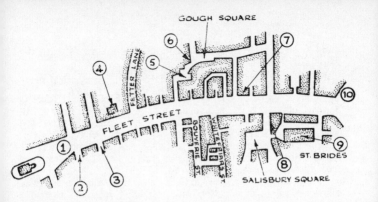

Walk 4. Fleet Street and its tributaries

1. Temple Bar
2. Middle Temple Lane
3. Prince Henry's Room
4. St. Dunstan's-in-the-West
5. Johnson's Court

6. Dr Johnson's house
7. Ye Olde Cheshire Cheese
8. Pepys plaque
9. St. Bride's
10. Edgar Wallace plaque

Staying just long enough to witness the free entertainment look now over the road to No. 37. This is **Hoare's Bank,** another very old-established private banking company. Like Child's it also retains its street sign, in this case a golden leather bottle, though some say it is really a leather wallet representing the lowly origins of the bank's founder, who, so the story goes, came to London with all his worldly possessions stowed away in such a purse. An old tradition here is that a member of the Hoare family always spent one night a week sleeping on the premises.

The bank's left-hand edge carries a 'blue plaque' indicating that the **Mitre Tavern** was once Hoare's next-door neighbour. This was one of the favourite haunts of Dr Johnson who in this pub once dandled some attractive Methodist maidens on his knees in an effort to win them away from their new-found faith! The Mitre was old in Johnson's time for Samuel Pepys went there twice in 1660. In 1788, four years after Johnson's death, the Mitre closed its doors.

We come next to **Fetter Lane,** possibly named after the beggars or fewters who once frequented it, or perhaps after the felt-makers or *feutriers.* On the other side of Fleet Street there is Mitre Court with its pub, previously Joe's Coffee House, but now bearing its new name almost like a memorial. This Court too is an entrance to the Temple. Then comes another opening, this time marked 'Sergeant's Inn', a memory of the time when the highest order of barristers, the sergeants-at-law, held court here until their society was dissolved in 1877.

Meanwhile, on the left (north) side of Fleet Street a series of alleyways awaits exploration and, on finding **Johnson's Court (5)** (the name has no connection with the Doctor), we follow the signs that take us to Gough Square and the delightful late-seventeenth century house **(6)** where Dr. Johnson lived for 10 years, many of them in great poverty. In the attic the great Dictionary, his literary triumph, was written and in this house too his wife died. The great conversationalist and wit, first Parliamentary journalist, poet and novelist who became Fleet Street's most famous personality, left this house in 1759. Ultimately he was given posthumously the greatest honour his country could offer, burial in Westminster Abbey.

Leave Gough Square by any of the alleys leading back to Fleet Street and then cross to the south side. We now turn into Bouverie Street passing the offices of *Punch* on our right and, beyond the entrance to the *News of the World,* the newspaper with the world's largest circulation, we shall find—with difficulty —**Magpie Alley.** Walk through and at the end turn left into Whitefriars Street; within a moment **Britten's Court** will be seen on the left. We stop here because below is the only surviving piece of the Whitefriars Monastery, in which lived the Carmelite Friars from 1241 to 1538. Strangely, the Act of Dissolution ordered by Henry VIII causing the monastic buildings to be demolished overlooked the 'right of sanctuary', and the area rapidly became the home of every sort of criminal. Known to Londoners as Alsatia, this unsavoury district, though destroyed in the Great Fire, was not to have the anomalous privilege of sanctuary removed for another 30 years.

Re-enter Fleet Street at the top of Whitefriars Street and almost opposite is the little entrance to the alley called Wine Office Court. Over its entrance you will see a lamp indicating that you have discovered Fleet Street's most eagerly sought-after pub, **Ye Olde Cheshire Cheese (7).** It was rebuilt in 1667 after the Great Fire, so many of the fixtures and fittings are of that date. Most taverns were built or rebuilt at this time because the city could not rise again unless its builders were provided with refreshment! The Cheshire Cheese claims a Dr. Johnson's chair, though it is unlikely he ever sat on it here, and in the cellar a bricked-up doorway hides an alleged tunnel under Fleet Street which, before the days of Henry VIII, allowed miscreants to seek sanctuary in the nearby Whitefriars Monastery.

Return to Fleet Street again and at **No. 147** you will see a statue that would make our earlier acquaintance, Queen Elizabeth I, turn in her grave: it is of Mary, Queen of Scots, who, at Elizabeth's command, spent 19 years in prison before being executed in 1587. The building here is called after her family name, Stuart House.

Continue down the hill, past the offices of the *Daily Telegraph* on the site of the Palace of the Bishops of Peterborough. Opposite is Salisbury Court, which we enter keeping a look-out for the blue plaque **(8)** on the side of the Reuter building which marks the birthplace of Samuel Pepys, civil servant and London's best known diarist. The little street opens into Salisbury Square, once the centre of the huge complex lived in by the Bishops of Salisbury.

This same side has a passageway leading directly into Fleet Street's most beautiful building—the church of **St. Bride's (9).** Believed to have given the western world its spire as a model for all wedding cakes, Wren's St. Bride's is the pride and joy of the Street. Arisen from the ashes of its pre-blitz predecessor, Wren would not fault any of the modern ideas incorporated in the renovations and would have been amazed at what the archaeologists found below. For here are the remains of all the earlier churches on the site as well as a portion of a Roman pavement and any visit to St. Bride's should really take in the crypt which has lately been turned into a museum of living history *in situ*. In this church Pepys was baptised, and Samuel Richardson, author of *Pamela*, was buried, as was the man who first brought printing to Fleet Street over 400 years ago—Caxton's pupil, Wynkyn de Worde.

The history of the United States is linked with St. Bride's too; apart from the spire's lightning conductor being the centre of a dispute between Benjamin Franklin and George III, there are also close associations with those who sailed away to become the founding fathers of the New England states.

St. Bride's, the 'parish church of the Press' receives the benevolence of all those who work in the street and this is reflected in the magnificent interior. For the passer-by however, it is the exterior, with the loftiest spire in the City, which dominates the scene.

Walk on now, past the graveyard with its burials piled high

above ground level; note on the left the rear of Ye Olde Bell, another tavern of 1667, and left into Fleet Street again. Opposite is **Poppins Court,** where once stood the London house of the Abbots of Cirencester, whose sign was the poppinjay. The commemorative stone, removed from over a former archway here, is now in the entrance lobby of the nearby Poppinjay public house.

At last we arrive at Ludgate Circus and the valley of the now sewered-up river Fleet. Turn left and you will immediately see the memorial plaque to **Edgar Wallace (10),** the Fleet Street journalist who wrote thrillers. He once sold papers here on the corner of the street which was to make him famous. Almost opposite was once the site of the notorious Fleet Prison, described in Dickens's *Pickwick Papers* and shown so vividly in Hogarth's *Rake's Progress*. Not least amongst its more famous prisoners was William Penn, Quaker and founder of Pennsylvania. Part of the London scene since the days of the Normans, destroyed during the Great Fire and again during the Gordon Riots of 1780, the Fleet Prison was not completely demolished until the 1840s. But no matter how buildings come and go Fleet Street and its tributaries will always attract the visitor.

St. James's Park Underground Station — Queen Anne's Gate — Dartmouth Street — Tothill Street — Broad Sanctuary — St. Margaret's Church — Old Palace Yard — Millbank — Dean Stanley Street — Smith Square — Lord North Street — Cowley Street — Barton Street — Great College Street — Dean's Yard — Westminster Abbey.

To most people's minds mention of Westminster Abbey will either bring back memories of coronations that have taken place there or remind them of the tombs and monuments of the famous within its walls. In fact the area around the Abbey is equally interesting; there are many intriguing places nearby normally missed by those who are overwhelmed by the Abbey itself.

Westminster Abbey has been on its present site for 900 years; indeed, if tradition is to be believed, a heathen temple here was converted to Christianity in the second and third century A.D. It stands on a one-time island in the estuary of one of London's lost rivers, the Tyburn, which rises in Hampstead and empties into the Thames near this spot. It was originally called Thorney Island because this was the nature of the place. Not, one would have thought, the best of neighbourhoods to build an abbey or, for that matter, a royal palace. The story is told that one evening two fishermen casting their nets in the Thames thereabouts were beckoned to by a figure on the southern shore. They went over to him, and he asked them for a passage across to Thorney Island. On the journey he revealed that he too was a fisherman and that he had come to dedicate the church that was to bear his name. It was, you see, St. Peter coming back to earth for the occasion! It is said that the Abbey was never consecrated by a mortal because of this event! Certainly the monks of Westminster put great store in the story by claiming a tithe—a tax—on all the fish caught in the river by Thorney Island. To-day the Abbey has much to offer students of history and architecture, showing as it does all the styles of the Gothic periods. However, we are not really concerned with the Abbey but the area surrounding it, through which we intend to walk.

The starting point for our walk is **St. James's Park Underground Station (1),** in itself an interesting building. It houses the headquarters of the London Transport Executive and carries one of the most famous telephone numbers in the London Telephone Directory—ABBey 1234, now 01-222 1234—from which you can get almost any information regarding transport in the London area. 'How long will it take me to get to . . .?', 'What

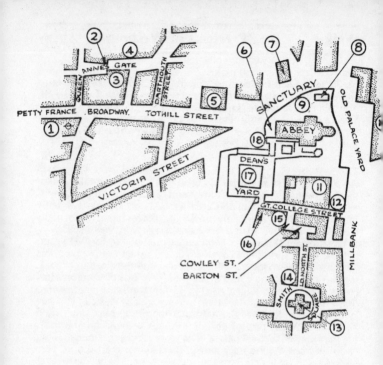

Walk 5. Precincts of Westminster Abbey

1. St. James's Park station
2. Queen Anne's Gate
3. Architectural Press
4. Palmerston plaque
5. United Nations plaque
6. Broad Sanctuary
7. Middlesex Guildhall
8. St. Margaret's church
9. Roman boundary stone
10. Houses of Parliament
11. Jewel Tower
12. Henry Moore sculpture
13. St. John the Evangelist
14. 'Air Raid Shelter' sign
15. T. E. Lawrence plaque
16. London House of St. Edward
17. Dean's Yard
18. Abbey Bookshop

is the time of the last train tonight from . . .?', 'Will you please send me a set of your maps and a collection of the many leaflets which will make my stay in London more profitable?' The building, to the design of Charles Holden, was erected in 1929 and the famous sculptors Jacob Epstein and Eric Gill were commissioned to do the figures on the outside.

The station's entrance is in the street called **Petty France.** This may have originated from the settlement of French refugees who came here after the signing of the Edict of Nantes in 1685, but there is the suggestion that the name is older by a century or more because of French wool merchants who lived here in the sixteenth century. Cross the road and walk towards Queen Anne's Gate pausing, after having crossed the road, to look back at the Holden building and noting how wide, by comparison, the roadway is at this junction. The street is called Broadway because with the construction of nearby Victoria Street in 1845 many small alleys and slums were swept away to make this splendid wide road.

Shortly **Queen Anne's Gate (2)** turns sharply to the right and one is immediately back in eighteenth century London. This is a street which shows the elegance of that age in its houses. Originally the first section had a brick wall at the far end and was known as Queen Square; beyond, where the road narrows slightly, was Park Street. Today they are one street. Take particular note of the key-stones of the arches over the windows. They are made of Coade Stone, an artificial substance manufactured by the Coade family at their factory which stood where the Royal Festival Hall now is on South Bank, near today's Waterloo Station. The formula of the compound was lost with the death of the last member of the family in the early nineteenth century. But the beauty of the work remains, and when one realises that many noted sculptors were involved in carving the moulds in which these stones were cast it is clear that the manufacturers strove for perfection. It is ironic too that modern scientists are unable to analyse the compound since Coade Stone is one of the few substances impervious to London's atmosphere. Note also the ornate overmantels of the doorways; these are often painted to look like stone or plasterwork.

Where the road narrows you will find a statue of Queen Anne. Originally it was to have graced a column at the west end of the church of St. Mary Le Strand which James Gibbs was then building. The Queen's death, however, on 1st August 1714, put an end to the idea. Instead, the church was given a steeple and Queen Anne's Gate got the statue.

A few doors along, at No. 9, are the offices of the **Architectural Press (3)**, in the basement of which can be found the only pub in

London that has no licence, and is therefore unable to serve liquor to the public. At the end of the last war large numbers of public houses were in ruins and many others were due for modernisation involving the destruction of their fine Victorian fixtures and fittings. John Betjeman, a great champion of Victoriana and at that time on the staff of the Press, urged the collection of all these wonderful bits and pieces and today they form part of the staff's lounge. Notice across the road a 'blue plaque' (4) indicating the birthplace of Lord Palmerston, Prime Minister of England.

At the end of Queen Anne's Gate turn right into Dartmouth Street and passing the Fabian Society headquarters on the right you will come to **Tothill Street.** A 'toothill' is a place suitable for a stronghold, and we read in the Authorised Version of the Bible how David in the Second Book of Samuel, 'took the totehill of Zion', which Wycliffe translates as the 'stronghold of Zion'. Tothill Fields has a long and sometimes macabre story to tell, the site being used for ordeals by battle, executions and burials. In the parochial accounts for the parish of St. John the Evangelist, Westminster, there is mention of '67 loads of soil for the graves of Tothill Fields wherein 1,200 Scotch prisoners taken in fight at the Battle of Worcester were buried'. In the fourteenth century the Gatehouse Prison was built on the Fields and here Sir Walter Raleigh spent the last night before his execution in 1618 in Old Palace Yard, Westminster. In 1690 Samuel Pepys, the famous diarist, was detained in the Gatehouse having been accused, falsely as it was later proved, of being 'affected to the King'. It was finally demolished in 1776, but not before having the wrath of Dr Johnson brought upon it for the foul condition in which the prisoners were kept.

At the end of Tothill Street one sees across the road Westminster Abbey in whose immediate precincts we have now arrived. Before crossing the road into the area of Sanctuary we should note the plaque (5) on the wall of the Methodist Central Hall, which informs us that this great hall was the venue for the early sessions of the United Nations Organisation. Built in the early part of this century in French Renaissance style, for the sum of £250,000, it has the third largest dome in London. In addition to the great central hall, which has seating for over 2,000 people, there are offices and banks into the side of the building. The late Sir Robert Perks, Liberal Member of Parliament and devout Methodist, was largely responsible for its construction. The site was previously occupied by the Aquarium, for many years a London pleasure haunt, but one which did not 'pay its way'.

Crossing the road, but keeping on the opposite side of the road from Westminster Abbey **(6)** we enter **Broad Sanctuary**. The first record of a sanctuary here was in the last quarter of the twelfth century. Briefly, a sanctuary was a place to which criminals could escape and live in 'safety', providing their crimes were not treasonable or anti-church. They had to agree to keep the Rules of the Sanctuary but apart from this were at liberty to come and go as they pleased. A now demolished street outside Sanctuary was called Thevenlane or Thieves Lane.

Cross the road towards the church which stands in the shadow of Westminster Abbey; look back for a moment and you will see the old **Middlesex Guildhall (7)** reminding us that Westminster was once the County City of the County of Middlesex. Just along on your right you will find the entrance to the churchyard of **St. Margaret's (8)**, parish church of Westminster. The original church was built at the time of Edward the Confessor, c. 1064, to accommodate the people of Westminster who had been sharing a part of the Abbey church with the monks, but with whom they were always quarrelling. The present building is of the early sixteenth century, and is an excellent example of a late Gothic church. Since 1614 St. Margaret's has been the parish church of the House of Commons and in 1735 Parliament assumed responsibility for some repairs that needed doing at that time. The windows commemorate people of a wide variety of talents. The West Window, given by Americans, shows scenes from the life of Raleigh who is buried near the High Altar; there are also memorial windows to Saxton the cartographer, Milton the poet, Admiral Blake the Puritan sea-dog who is buried in the church-yard (his grave is unmarked), and many others. But perhaps the most curious and interesting of all is the East Window of Flemish glass. It was a gift for Henry VII from Ferdinand and Isabella of Spain, whose daughter Catherine of Aragon married Henry's eldest son, Prince Arthur. Later, when Arthur died, Catherine became the wife of Arthur's brother, Henry VIII. Prince Arthur and Catherine are shown in the bottom half of the window, but neither saw their portraits here. After passing through a number of hands Parliament purchased the window in 1758 and installed it in its own church. By the side of the west tower is the modern porch and opposite in the grass of the churchyard you will discover a **Roman boundary stone (9)** embedded in the ground. It has the Roman numeral IV on it, and quite what it is intended to mark nobody is sure.

Taking the pathway with St. Margaret's on your left and the Abbey on your right, you will come to **St. Margaret's Street;** turn right and, passing the eastern chapels of the Abbey on your right, you will come to the statue of George V opposite Old Palace Yard. Look across the Yard at the vast expanse of what was formerly the Royal Palace of St. Stephen at Westminster, now more popularly called the **Houses of Parliament (10).**

Opposite the tall Victoria Tower on your right you will find, set back from the road, the **Jewel Tower (11).** Thought by some to have been the Abbot of Westminster's prison, its uses over the past 700 years have been various. It certainly must have formed part of the old Palace, destroyed by fire in 1834, because in the fourteenth century it was used as a depository for the private jewels and treasure of Edward III. Much later it became a storage-house for the records of the House of Lords, and in the nineteenth century the Tower was used by the Weights and Measures Department. The roof was destroyed in the last war, but since then the whole building has been restored and fish once more swim in its clear waters. The Tower is open to visitors throughout the year.

We walk on, passing on the left the Victoria Tower Gardens with the statue of Mrs Pankhurst, great champion of 'Votes for Women', and further back a replica of Rodin's famous sculpture *The Burghers of Calais*. We shall also see, on our right, a fine abstract by Henry Moore **(12).**

Soon we reach Dean Stanley Street, and there turn right, shortly to find ourselves in **Smith Square**, dominated by Thomas Archer's church of **St. John the Evangelist, Westminster (13).** It was built in 1728 as one of the Fifty New Churches of Queen Anne's reign. Dickens, in *Our Mutual Friend*, describes the church 'generally resembling some petrified monster, frightful and gigantic on its back with its legs in the air'. There is the story that when asked what sort of church she would like the architect to build, Queen Anne kicked over a stool and said 'Build me one like that!'. Actually the four corner towers support the rest of the building between them and, bearing in mind that this land is very marshy, it is not surprising that Archer had to use such methods to stop the church from sinking into what had once been the river bank.

Turning to the right when entering the square one can walk round two sides of the church, and at the same time admire the lovely remaining eighteenth century houses.

One of the ways out of the square is by the charming eighteenth century Lord North Street. Note the 'Public Air Raid Shelter' sign on the first left-hand house **(14).** There are several more such signs in the street.

Lord North Street crosses Great Peter Street, leads into Cowley Street and then into Barton Street. Note, towards the end of this last, on the left-hand side, the blue plaque commemorating Lawrence of Arabia **(15),** who lived in this house until his untimely death in a motor-cycle accident.

This trio of streets leads us to Great College Street, and looking to the right, one sees the outside wall of the old monastic precinct of Westminster Abbey. Turn left and you will be passing alongside one of the many monastic houses in London today—the red brick **London House of St. Edward (16)**, of the Society of St. John the Evangelist. This is the oldest Order for men of the Church of England, having been founded in the latter part of the nineteenth century; thus within the shadow of the old Abbey of Westminster thrives a new monastery! Immediately opposite is a pair of iron gates leading into **Dean's Yard (17)**, part of the jurisdiction of the Abbey. Dean's Yard contains, amongst other places, Church House, the Parliament House of the Church of England, and Westminster School, a famous London public school. The boys play cricket or football, according to season, on the centre grass plot—out-of-bounds to visitors. In the far corner of the Yard there is a gatehouse. Pass through this and you will find yourself at the west end of Westminster Abbey, and close to the **Abbey Bookshop (18)**, which, after having walked around the Abbey's precincts, is well worth a visit.

Walk 6   In the steps of the Blackfriars

Blackfriars Underground Station — Mermaid Theatre — Upper Thames Street — St. Benet's Hill — Queen Victoria Street — Godliman Street — Knightrider Street — Carter Lane — Dean's Court — Wardrobe Place — St. Andrew's Hill — Ireland Yard — Playhouse Yard — Church Entry — Carter Lane — Blackfriars Lane — The Black Friar public house.

In the early part of the thirteenth century a group of black-robed friars attached to the Order of St. Dominic settled in London on land now occupied by Lincoln's Inn. By 1276 they had become a prosperous community and moved to a larger site at Thames-side adjacent to Baynard's Castle. There they built a church, cloisters and other priory buildings; later they even had their own quay. Highly favoured by Edward I who buried the heart of his Queen Eleanor within the precincts (the rest of her was put in Westminster Abbey!) not a few noble, even royal, figures were to have their mortal remains interred at Blackfriars. On three occasions Parliament met within its walls; one of them, in 1523, being the session when Sir Thomas More was made

Speaker; More was also present at the so-called Black Parliament of 1529 which took place at the Priory when, for the first time, he clashed with Henry VIII over the latter's proposals for a divorce from Catherine of Aragon. Within four years Black Friars were being executed over the same issue and in 1538 the end came with the priory's surrender. From that time until its destruction during the Great Fire of 1666, the priory buildings and lands were in the possession of the nobility and their sub-tenants, some of whom we shall become acquainted with on the walk.

Using **Blackfriars Underground Station** to start from, immediately left can be seen the widest road bridge **(1)** across the Thames, opened in 1869 by Queen Victoria whose statue is nearby. Although London has had other bridges built since then none has been as wide as Blackfriars—a rather sad commentary on progress!

Leave the station by turning right and you soon come to **Blackfriars Station (Southern Region) (2)**. This newly rebuilt terminus and offices overlook the river and the Castle Baynard development.

Continue past the station, cross the little road and, keeping the railings on your right, use the subway to enter Upper Thames Street. On the immediate right is the **Mermaid Theatre (3)**, a venture started in 1959 by actor-producer Bernard Miles. The Mermaid is the only permanent theatre in the City of London and is, indeed, the first to be there since the sixteenth century. Patronised financially by the City Corporation and the odd business house, its plays are performed in what was an old warehouse-cum-prison serving the adjacent Puddle Dock. The conversion to a theatre is a brilliant piece of design and the architect retained the shell of the building as well as its entrance of massive cast-iron Doric columns.

Incidentally, both this street and its eastern partner, Lower Thames Street, follow the line of the Roman riverside defensive wall. Almost every excavation along this Roman thoroughfare has yielded enormous amounts of archaeological material, indicating that the Romans had built many villas by the Thames.

After the Norman Conquest this section of the riverside was occupied by the gaunt and forbidding Baynard's Castle. Not so well-known as the Tower, it was one of three strong fortifications (the other was Montefichett Castle) built to defend and protect Norman London. Originally built by one Ralph Baynard, a henchman of William the Conqueror, this castle only lasted until 1212 when it was deliberately demolished by King John after its rebellious owner had fled for his life. On returning to favour, the ex-miscreant rebuilt the place. In 1278 the castle was sold to the Black Friars, but early in the 1400s it was burnt down. Baynard's

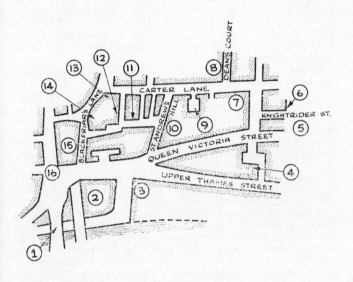

Walk 6. In the steps of the Blackfriars

1. Blackfriars Bridge
2. Blackfriars Station
3. Mermaid Theatre
4. St. Benet's church
5. College of Arms
6. Horn Tavern
7. Shakespeare plaque
8. St. Paul's Deanery
9. Wardrobe Place
10. St. Andrew-by-the-Wardrobe
11. Priory remains
12. St. Ann's graveyard
13. Priory plaque
14. Society of Apothecaries
15. Market arches
16. Black Friar tavern

Castle was rebuilt again, this time a little further east, and in it Edward IV was proclaimed King of England. It continued to play a reasonably active role until the Great Fire of London when it was partially destroyed. The site was not fully cleared until the 1880s. Previous to the recent Upper Thames Street demolitions a blue plaque commemorated the castle as indeed a local public house still does.

Continue along the street for a hundred yards and on the left we reach the pretty red brick church of **St. Benet's (4)** (1677–85) decorated with festoons and topped with hipped roofs. One feels that Christopher Wren put a great deal of affection into its design. The previous church was where Inigo Jones, the seventeenth century architect, was buried and one ponders over the reason why Wren saw fit not to perpetuate the memory of his great predecessor. Since 1879 St. Benet's has been used by the London Welsh Episcopalians.

Using the stairs that connect the embankment with the new roadway, we arrive in **Queen Victoria Street,** opposite Faraday House, the International Telephone Exchange.

Turn right and in a few yards cross this main road to the **College of Arms (5),** fronted by a magnificent pair of gates picked out in black and gold, presented to the College in 1956 by an American benefactor. The College is a tight corporation consisting of three Kings of Arms (Garter, Clarenceux and Norroy & Ulster) who are assisted by six Heralds (York, Richmond, Windsor, Somerset, Lancaster and Chester) and four Pursuivants bearing the romantic titles of Portcullis, Rouge Dragon, Rouge Croix and Bluemantle. They work under the direction of the Earl Marshal of England, traditionally, since 1672, the Duke of Norfolk, even though he is not a member of the College. They arrange state ceremonials, design coats of arms, check pedigrees and family trees and work in all those fields where heraldry still holds court. Their attractive building in mellow red brick dates from 1671 being one of the tiny handful of non-religious post-Great Fire buildings to survive. The site was originally occupied by Derby House which was acquired by the College of Arms in 1553.

Leave the College on your right, turn right into Godliman Street and again right into **Knightrider Street.** This is a very old name, first heard of in a document of 1332, perhaps derived from the route taken by the knights who, fully armed for the tournament, would come along here from the Tower on their way to the jousting grounds at Smithfield. However, our reason for entering Knightrider Street is to see the **Horn Tavern (6),** a delightful old pub which seems to occupy most of the street. It was well-known to Charles Dickens, who, in *Pickwick Papers*, made it a venue of

Messrs Snodgrass, Tupman and Winkle when they came here to purchase a bottle or two of good wine which they afterwards took to the nearby Newgate Prison where Mr Pickwick was temporarily incarcerated. The Horn has changed but little since then and is well worth a visit if the time can be spared.

Walk back to Godliman Street, turn right and then left into Carter Lane. After a few yards you will find a wall (at right angles to the pavement) upon which is a plaque (7) reminding us that William Shakespeare was resident in this district. This is merely the first indication of Shakespeare's presence in the precincts of Blackfriars.

Carter Lane is very narrow, with numerous sub-streets and alleys leading off. One feels that this sector was left untouched by the Great Fire and this is how London used to be. But Wren's grandiose schemes were ignored and much of London was rebuilt without any alteration to the street plan. Only the houses were different, built more of brick than timber. Now, much of this district is to disappear in a new wave of town planning, and walking amidst the many empty buildings around here one is perhaps taking a last look at old London.

A few yards past the Shakespeare plaque turn right into **Dean's Court.** Here, on the left, behind two gates often left open, is the Deanery of St. Paul's Cathedral (8), a delightful, well-proportioned, 1670 Wren house, its door-case framed with garlands—a very picturesque scene spoilt only by the general gloominess of the immediate surroundings.

Back down Carter Lane again, turn right. On our right is a very long building with a grubby exterior but bearing on its walls signs of its former glory. This was once the St. Paul's Choir School in a style that Sir Nikolaus Pevsner jokingly calls 'South Kensington'. The external walls were embellished with religious motifs and floral decoration not unlike the sort of thing one sees in Northern Italy—ideal for a sunny clime but not for the smoke-begrimed London of the mid-1870s.

Look now for No. 57 Carter Lane a little further on (it is opposite the Choir School) and there you will find an entrance into **Wardrobe Place (9).** This humble-looking oasis endeavouring, as it were, to escape the squalor of its environs, has a history worthy of its attempts to survive. For here in medieval times was the King's Wardrobe, established by Edward III, where were kept the ceremonial robes of state, on view to the public just as the Crown Jewels are today. Therefore it was, in a way, a museum though it seemed to have another and more mysterious role, because in 1604 William Shakespeare received 4½ yards of scarlet cloth from the Wardrobe enabling him to attend the state entry into London of James I. Samuel Pepys, too, was a visitor to the Wardrobe on more than one occasion though he must have been among the last because in 1666 the building was destroyed in the Great Fire, and not rebuilt. In 1709 the office of the Wardrobe was abolished and the garden of the great house was converted into this nice little courtyard.

Into Carter Lane again, turn left, and left into St. Andrew's Hill, past the elegant eighteenth century rectory on the left to the church of **St. Andrew-by-the-Wardrobe (10)**, a few yards further on. This is another Wren church, of 1692. In its early days it was called St. Andrew's-by-the-Castle, referring to **Baynard's Castle.** Like so many of Wren's buildings in red brick it is very attractive and our view of it, so close to the rear, is by no means the best. It is a High Church, both spiritually and physically, the latter due to the 1869–1871 cutting of Queen Victoria Street which left the building perched so high above pavement level. St. Andrew's was gutted by incendiary bombs during the last war but it has since been beautifully restored.

Return to St. Andrew's Hill. On the left is **Ireland Yard,** which we enter. We are now in the depths of what was once the Black-friars Priory complex. This alley is named after William Ireland, one of the sub-tenants of the previously dissolved priory buildings. On the right there is a small clearing in which can be seen the only remaining piece of the great priory left above ground **(11)**. An inscription on the garden's outside wall tells us this was once part of the priory's dorter or dormitory.

Ireland Yard opens into **Playhouse Yard;** this is all that remains of the famed Blackfriars Theatre. Opening in 1577 as London's second official playhouse it has often been confused with the better known and slightly later Blackfriars Theatre of James Burbage. The latter building occupied the so-called Parliament Chamber of the Priory and from its start met with opposition from its aristocratic neighbours. Later, James's son Richard took over both the building and the players, as part of a syndicate which included John Hemming, Henry Condell and William Shakespeare. Certainly the latter had most of his plays performed here. The Blackfriars Theatre became the winter home of the group; in the summer they played at the Globe on the other side of the river. By 1642 the Puritans had gained control of the area and the Blackfriars was ordered to close down; in 1655 the theatre was demolished.

Just before entering Playhouse Yard we would have seen a little alley called Church Entry. A few yards up there is the little graveyard of **St. Ann's, Blackfriars (12)** (another fragment of the same churchyard was the clearing off Ireland's Yard). **St.** Ann's was originally the parish church of the precincts of the priory. During the period when the theatre was nextdoor a constant stream of complaints was made to the Burbages about the theatre's trumpets, drums and acclamations drowning the services. The church perished in the Great Fire and was never rebuilt. Oddly enough, in 1905, the famous architect Banister Fletcher was commissioned to build a new St. Ann's Vestry Hall in Edwardian Baroque style a yard or two away.

Go now to the top of Church Entry, left into Carter Lane and left into Blackfriars Lane, passing a blue plaque (13) to Blackfriars Priory on your left. Some little way down, on your left, is the entrance to the Hall of the City Livery Company, the **Society of Apothecaries (14),** in a building of 1670 and 1786 containing a very beautiful main hall in panelled black oak. This was one of the very few company halls to survive the Blitz. The Apothecaries used to be classed with the Grocers because of their background of herbs and suchlike remedies, but as time passed a real division occurred and in 1617 they received a Royal Charter. Since the nineteenth century the Society has been able to act as an examining body in Medicine and Surgery and in consequence a Licentiate of the Society is qualified to be a general practitioner. Their coat of arms, seen over the doorway, is surmounted by a rhinoceros and is supported by two unicorns, the horns of both beasts being highly prized for their medicinal properties.

We now make our way down **Blackfriars Lane.** Keep a look-out, though, for a series of arches (15) on the right-hand side of the Lane, each of which has a stone symbol of the trade once carried on within each arch; a pig's head, a fish, a piece of turnery and other objects are included, made in what appears to be imperishable Coade Stone.

At the end, turn right into Queen Victoria Street, and just past the railway bridge on the right is London's most highly decorated pub—**The Black Friar (16).** Covered from top to bottom in Art Nouveau by H. Fuller Clark and Henry Poole, the theme, inside and out, is of conviviality and jolly friars. There is even one fat friar pointing the way to the Saloon Bar. Which perhaps, is not such a bad idea!

Walk 7   Mayfair—on the course of the Tyburn

Green Park Underground Station — Piccadilly — Whitehorse Street — Shepherd Market — Curzon Street — Queen Street, Mayfair — Charles Street — Berkeley Square — Hill Street — Farm Street — South Audley Street — Grosvenor Square.

During the first two weeks of May, from 1688 until 1760, a fair was held in a suburban London field which was to stamp its name on the richest square mile in all Britain outside the City of London. From its earliest days, even before it was transferred from the Haymarket, the fair was notorious for wantonness and in its later years was to be called 'a nursery of Vice and Atheism'. The great development of the West End during the mid-eighteenth century brought about its eventual closure, for the wealthy and influential citizens who came to live within earshot were able to nullify even a fair held under the rights of a Royal Charter. Thus Mayfair began to change to its present form, though many of the fair's features survived and on the walk a sharp eye will soon detect them!

Starting from **Green Park Underground Station,** we walk along Piccadilly towards Hyde Park Corner keeping the park on our left. The name of this roadway has somewhat cloudy origins; but the Middlesex county records of 1623 tell us that there was a large house near today's Piccadilly Circus belonging to a Mr George Baker, a tailor. He sold at his shop a fashionable accessory called a pickadil—a sort of ruff sometimes worn on the collar or about the hem of a garment. Soon his house became known as Piccadilly Hall.

It was only one of the many large mansions that lined the road to Hyde Park. Indeed, the Green Park Station is on the site of a great house which once belonged to the Duke of Devonshire. The second street along is Clarges Street. Turn in a yard or two and on the right at No. 1 is the **Kennel Club,** the repository of every canine pedigree in the United Kingdom and elsewhere.

Back into Piccadilly, turn right, and on the Park side of the road we can see a magnificent pair of wrought-iron gates, picked out in blue and gold. In the early eighteenth century they fronted Lord Heathfield's house at Turnham Green, but in 1837 were purchased by the Duke of Devonshire to gate his exquisite Chiswick House. He later fixed them to the frontage of his Piccadilly mansion and in 1921, just prior to demolition, the gate became part of Green Park's railings.

Crossing Half Moon Street a few yards further on is one of the great Piccadilly landmarks popularly known, because of the

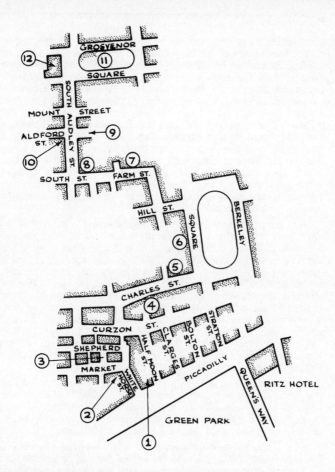

Walk 7. Mayfair—on the course of the Tyburn

1. Naval and Military Club
2. Antique shop
3. Shepherd Market
4. Dartmouth House
5. Running Footman
6. Clive of India's house
7. Church of the Immaculate Conception
8. Goodes
9. Grosvenor Chapel
10. Purdey's
11. Grosvenor Square
12. U.S. Embassy

giant lettering on the gateposts, as the IN and OUT Club, but in reality the **Naval and Military Club (1)**. This typical example of a West End town house dates from 1756–1760 and was once lived in by the Duke of Cambridge and, later, by Queen Victoria's Prime Minister, Lord Palmerston. We see only the frontage. Continuing down the slope of the Tyburn valley, Whitehorse Street is reached. As we turn into it, the first doorway on the right (95 Piccadilly) is the entrance to the **American Club,** before 1919 the home of Sir Bertram and Lady Falle. She, being a Bostonian, sold the house to her compatriots and it has since become the meeting place for London's American businessmen. It was here that visiting Mayor of New York, Jimmy Walker, when given the floor at a dinner in his honour, remarked: 'As Napoleon said to Josephine on entering her boudoir, I am not coming here to speak!'

One immediately notices that **Whitehorse Street** is out of character with the rest of Piccadilly's side streets. Narrow and winding, it follows the course of a now disappeared tributary of the Thames—the river Tyburn. Though very small it played a large part in London's history, its estuary forming two arms between which Westminster Abbey was sited. It rises in Hampstead on the northern rim of the London Basin, forms a lake in Regent's Park, crosses Oxford Street—at which point in medieval days it was tapped to provide the City of London with some of its water supply, shapes not a few of Mayfair's streets including Whitehorse Street, forms the valley of the western end of Piccadilly, flows under Green Park and below Buckingham Palace and on to the Thames at Westminster.

Whitehorse Street has little to offer. But towards the end of the street can be found the antique shop owned by Denisa, the Lady Newborough (2), a remarkable woman who has been quoted as saying 'I sell only what I know about, and I never sell anything to anyone if I don't like the look of them'.

Now Whitehorse Street opens out into **Shepherd Market (3)**, the very heart of Mayfair and the site of the earlier charter fair. Consisting of the minute square we are now in, an even tinier piazza and a few surrounding streets, it is Piccadilly's quaintest backwater. Owned, designed and laid out in 1735–1746 by Edward Shepherd, it is a reminder of how carefully the eighteenth century speculators considered their tenants. Shops, a market, a chapel (now gone) and taverns. A petite self-contained village it was and still remains. Not so long ago it was one of the most notorious 'red-light' districts in London, until the Act of Parliament swept 'the girls' off the street. Despite the changes Shepherd Market is still one of the great off-beat sights of

London, picturesque and lively, with pretty little restaurants and a fascinating street life if we are to include the many tourists who flock here just to take photographs. And if you have time to spare, have a drink in Shepherd's and perhaps a meal in Tiddy Dol's.

Now go through one of the two archways and enter **Curzon Street.** Opposite will be seen a most irreverent-looking Third Church of Christ, Scientist, as well as two adjoining and interesting little shops. The first is Trumper's, the gentlemen's hairdresser, unique in its austere, not over-modern, window display and the three coats of arms, indicating that Royal haircuts have been provided. The other is Heywood Hill, the bookseller, considered the home of the literary establishment, where many notables obtain their current reading. Here once worked Nancy Mitford, of U and non-U fame.

Turn left, cross Curzon Street and enter **Queen Street, Mayfair** (This is the proper name of the street—to omit the affix would create confusion!). No. 6, on the right, was once the home of Mrs Fitzgeorge, a lady of some importance who greatly disturbed Queen Victoria. As Louisa Fairbrother, a 'light entertainer', she was secretly to marry Prince George, heir to the Duke of Cambridge. The Queen was furious, but was unable to invoke the Royal Marriage Act, as her discovery was three sons too late! So the sons were disallowed title inheritances; reference books failed to mention Mrs Fitzgeorge, as she was called and since the ducal home was barred, they lived in Queen Street, Mayfair. She died in 1890 after 50 years of happy marriage. Only in 1935 did the Royal Family ever visit No. 6, when Queen Mary came to sort out the heirlooms of this morganatic marriage.

At the top of Queen Street, Mayfair, turn right into **Charles Street,** which epitomises the whole area—enormous eighteenth century houses with plain, even dirty-black exteriors, but sumptuously decorated interiors. Distinctly aristocratic, they are still lived in by people of immense wealth who prefer a town house in the West End rather than a large house in Hampstead, Kensington or Belgravia.

No. 37, on the right, is **Dartmouth House (4),** the London headquarters of the English-Speaking Union. Originally three houses, it was converted in 1890 by Lord Revelstoke into one very large mansion. Note the nice architectural trimmings and some fine ironwork. The English-Speaking Union has been here since 1918 and exists to draw together and give assistance to all those who speak our common tongue.

Further along on the left, on the corner of Hays Mews, we come to a pub whose name is unique. **'I am the only Running Footman'** (5) says the sign, and that's the official title. It was the job of this personal servant to run ahead of a nobleman's coach, to pay tolls, assist passengers to alight and at night to carry the flare. He could run at seven miles an hour and would refresh himself from the top of his wand which carried wine and egg-whites. Such menials were common enough in the seventeenth century but this pub commemorates the last of them. The fourth Lord Queensbury, who gave this place its name and who died in 1810, was the last nobleman to exploit his servants in this wretched manner.

Continue along Charles Street and at the end, where we turn left, we are in lovely Berkeley Square. The massive plane trees, some of the largest in London, were planted in 1789 and somewhere in their branches sings the allegorical nightingale. The square is called after the Berkeley family who owned much of this part of the West End in the seventeenth century. There was a time when it was purely residential and as such exceeded Grosvenor Square for sheer wealth. Now, the residents have all gone and only a few of the old noble houses remain. Walking up the gentle slope of the Tyburn valley, and noting the fine iron-work outside some of the older houses, we come to **No. 45–46 (6)**, a pair of good stone-faced buildings believed to have been designed by William Chambers, an architect of the Georgian Golden Age. Clive of India lived here, as the blue plaque denotes, as did Henry Flitcroft, another great Georgian. William Kent was responsible for **No. 44**, considered to be the finest terrace house in London, and though the exterior now looks as new as the day it was built, it gives the passer-by no idea of the splendour within. Inside there is the grandest of grand-staircases, to say the least of many beautiful rooms. Kent built this house in 1742–1744 for Lady Isabella Finch, though today it has become the Clermont Club, sometimes known as Aspinall's, where, should you wish, you can lose £50,000 in style. In short, it is the most aristocratic gambling club in all England. Even the basement has a glory of its own, for here is Annabel's, a night-spot for top people.

Turn left into Hill Street, and then right into Farm Street, following it round to the left. Farm Street is basically a mews, where once the nobility kept their horses, carriages and coachmen in cottages. The twentieth century, however, has seen these properties converted at enormous cost into the most dazzling of small town houses. The result is that Farm Street is now well worth lingering in.

We have now entered the estate of the Grosvenors, which

family came into possession of these parts in 1677 when Sir Thomas Grosvenor, Baronet of Eaton Boat, at 21 years of age married Mary Davies, aged 12 years and 8 months, heiress to the fabulously wealthy Audleys. The marriage laid the foundation of the largest and richest estate in Westminster. As long ago as 1880 their descendants were drawing £1,000 a day in ground rent, though their Mayfair lands were but a small portion of their total holdings.

Farm Street has, on the right, two buildings of interest. The first bears over its doorway a large coloured coat of arms of the City of Westminster and serves as one of that Council's street cleansing depots! The second, the greystone **Church of the Immaculate Conception (7)** is of more than usual interest. Here is no ordinary Catholic place of worship, for this is the London church of the Jesuit Fathers, an order of great importance within the Catholic body politic. Built in 1844–1849 by J. J. Scholes, with a high altar by the famous Pugin, the church has a superb interior, numerous chapels of great beauty and an east window in stained glass by Evie Hone (1953).

Continue into South Street and turn right at South Audley Street. At this corner is **Goodes (8)**—a china and glassware shop that claims to be the largest in the world. Certainly it is one of the more impressive Mayfair businesses, and is typical of many in this area in that it is run by a dynasty. Founded in 1827 by an ex-tax-collector, William Goode, the shop is now controlled by the great-grandson. The main entrance has a very clever mechanical device which throws the doors open when the step is trodden on, pre-dating our modern electric-eye gadgets by a half century or so. It is often referred to as the 'Elephant Shop' because of the two richly decorated china elephants to be seen in the windows. They were made by Minton for Messrs. Goode and shown at the Paris Exhibition of 1889. The family have resisted all offers to sell them.

On the next block will be seen (best viewed from across the road) the simple and homely **Grosvenor Chapel (9)**. Originally a so-called proprietory chapel, this was built by Benjamin Timbrell in 1730 as part of the great Grosvenor Square scheme. Such chapels were built as a speculation based on pew-rents; they were not usually consecrated and Holy Communion could only be celebrated by licence from the local bishop. This one seems thoroughly out of place, looking as if it should be in New England. Indeed, the style is called Colonial, and one feels that when the American servicemen worshipped here during the Second World War they must have felt very homesick. Earlier regulars included the elderly Florence Nightingale, who lived around the corner in South Street. The vaults, sealed for 100

years and their exact whereabouts a mystery, contain the remains
of John Wilkes, who fought for the liberty of Englishmen, and of
Lady Mary Wortley Montague, writer, wit and friend of Pope,
Addison and other notable literary and society leaders.

Opposite at No. 57 is a local curiosity—**Purdey's the gun-
makers (10).** This is another dynastic business brought here
from Oxford Street in 1826 by James Purdey, he being persuaded
to do so by the first Duke of Westminster who was one of the
Grosvenors. James built this place as a picture-gallery just in
case the gun business failed. However, guns were a great success,
but the Long Room, as it is called, is a gallery filled with portraits
of four generations of aristocratic customers and appears to be
a delightful compromise.

Finally, we enter **Grosvenor Square (11)** which with its six
acres is London's largest. It was laid out in 1695 by Richard
Grosvenor, occupying the site of Oliver's Mount, an earthwork
thrown up for the defence of London when Charles I was
advancing after his Edgehill victory (hence, nearby Mount
Street). By 1725 the square had been filled with very large houses
and extremely wealthy tenants.

Grosvenor Square has long been associated with Americans,
and one of the first residents during the years 1731–1743 was
Charles Calvert, fifth Lord Baltimore and the hereditary proprietor of Maryland. But the first genuine American to live in
the square was John Adams, later President of the United States,
though when he and his daughter Abigail lived at **No. 9** (which
house is still standing) he was then only America's first minister
to Britain. From then on the square became a favourite place for
visiting Americans, the peak being reached during the Second
World War when it was tagged 'Eisenhowerplatz'. Because of
these associations the square was chosen as the site for W. Reid
Dick's statue of Franklin Delano Roosevelt and the fine likeness
was unveiled by Mrs Roosevelt in 1948 in the presence of
George VI.

During the late 1950s the whole west side was demolished to
make room for Eero Saarinen's massive **U.S. Embassy (12),** a
very good piece of modern diplomatic architecture spoiled only
by the 35 foot long eagle spreading itself on the roof's edge.

The Monument — Monument Street — St. Mary at Hill —
Eastcheap — Philpot Lane — Lime Street — Leadenhall Market
— Leadenhall Street — Cornhill — St. Peter's Church — St.
Michael's Church — St. Michael's Alley — Castle Court — Ball
Court — Birchin Lane — Change Alley — Lombard Street —
King William Street — The Monument.

On the night of 1st September 1666, Thomas Farynor, one of
the King's bakers, went to bed little realising that he was to play
an important part in the history of the City of London. He was
awakened, some two hours later, by thick clouds of smoke
pouring into his bedroom from the bakery downstairs. His
daughter and maidservant sleeping in other rooms nearby were
also disturbed in their sleep. The bakery was on fire . . . Farynor
saw that their way of escape down the stairway was impossible,
so he took them to the upper rooms of the house and they made
their escape through an attic window. The little maidservant was
too terrified to jump on to the roof of the next house, and so
became the Fire's first victim.

It had been a dry summer, and soon, with the help of a fierce
wind to the east, neighbouring houses caught fire; shortly after,
the whole street was ablaze. The fact that a nearby inn had a
stack of dry hay in its courtyard did not help matters.

Meanwhile, the fire had attracted the attention of some city
officials including the Lord Mayor, Sir Thomas Bludworth, who
was reported as saying 'a woman might piss it out. . . .' In fairness
to the Lord Mayor fires were no new thing for the city; the past
history of the city was full of them, but, as he was later to realise,
this was to be no ordinary fire.

Another noted citizen wakened by the fire was Samuel Pepys,
whose diary entries for this period contained some of the finest
descriptions, but he too regarded it as just another fire and went
back to bed.

Next morning, however, the situation had worsened, and
people were beginning to take a serious view of the fire. In fact,
it was to rage for three days and three nights before it was
contained, and even then there were further small outbreaks
over the period of the next week or so. One later diarist recorded,
a year later, that smouldering timbers were still being found
buried under the rubble of what had once been the very fine and
noble City of London.

The Great Fire made thousands of people homeless, burned
five-sixths of the city, and caused many to think again about the

47

so-called fire precautions of London. It also gave a golden opportunity to 'that miracle of youth, Doctor Christopher Wren', as Evelyn described him, to formulate plans for a new City of London. Even before the flames of the fires had abated Wren was presenting his plans for the city's rebuilding to King Charles II. So did several other 'amateur architects', but to no avail; their plans did not even reach the city fathers for consideration. But what did emerge from this Great Fire was a series of beautiful, rebuilt churches and a magnificent St. Paul's Cathedral, all in the new Renaissance style of architecture.

To walk from one extreme of the fire to the other would take too long, but to explore the area that the fire consumed in the first 24 hours is far more practicable.

Let us begin this walk at the **Monument (1),** just a few yards away from the Monument Underground Station, in itself a constant reminder of the Great Fire of 1666. It stands 202 feet high, which is the distance from its base to the site of the house in Pudding Lane where the fire started, and is the work, basically, of Sir Christopher Wren. Built between 1671 and 1677 it is a fluted Doric column of Portland stone, and the view from the top is still one of the finest in London. It is necessary to climb 311 stairs to reach the balcony. Nowadays this is enclosed and has been since, amongst others, two bakers and a baker's daughter committed suicide by throwing themselves from the top! An ironic twist of history! Explore around the base of the column and you will find a bas-relief, by Cauis Gabriel Cibber, representing London, her destruction and how she will rise again from the ashes of the Great Fire.

Returning to the entrance of the column let us leave the Monument behind us and walk down Monument Street, pausing when we reach **Pudding Lane (2)** to note this insignificant by-way of the city which played such an important part in its story. Continuing, we come to the **Cock (3)** public house, where we read, perhaps enviously, that those engaged in business in the nearby Billingsgate Fish Market may obtain a drink here prior to normal opening hours. Next-door once stood a cafe where the fish-porters could get a warm dish of soup, taken from a copper that was never allowed to run dry, always being replenished before it could do so. The soup was delicious! One day the sign 'Under New Management' was posted in the window, and very soon the copper of soup was allowed to run dry. There, in the bottom of the vessel, was an old fish-porter's hat which was promptly removed. The soup never tasted the same. . . . This hat was the sort that can still be seen on the heads of the fish-porters of Billingsgate today. Made of wood, lined with leather, they protect the porters when carrying the

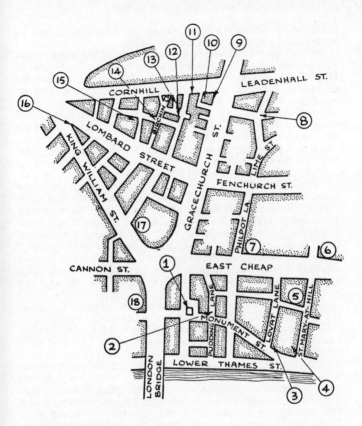

Walk 8. Great Fire of London

1. The Monument
2. Pudding Lane
3. Cock tavern
4. Watermen's Hall
5. St. Mary at Hill
6. St. Margaret Pattens
7. Mice carving
8. Leadenhall Market
9. Standard of Cornhill plaque
10. St. Peter-upon-Cornhill
11. St. Michael's, Cornhill
12. George and Vulture
13. Simpson's Chop House
14. Birchin Lane
15. Garraway's plaque
16. St. Mary Woolnoth
17. St. Clement, Eastcheap
18. Square Rigger

heavy boxes of fish. They are almost exactly the same hats as were worn by archers in the field of battle.

We have now reached **Lower Thames Street** and the junction with St. Mary at Hill. Just a few yards up the latter one finds the **Hall of the Company of Watermen and Lightermen of the City of London (4).** Founded in the sixteenth century to protect all those whose livelihood directly depended on the river, this well-preserved hall dates from 1786 and is in the style of Adam and Wyatt. On its coat of arms can be seen the crossed oars and the long row-boat used by the watermen and two sacks representing the goods which they would unload from the ships at anchor in the Thames.

Walking up **St. Mary at Hill** one soon comes to the church (5) which gives its name to the street. Although not destroyed in the Great Fire it was rebuilt in the latter half of the eighteenth century. John Stow, in his Survey of the cities of London and Westminster, says that St. Thomas à Becket, London's own saint, was rector here for a time in the twelfth century. Another, though much later, rector was Prebendary Wilson Carlile, founder of the Church Army. Today the church is the home of the Christian Evidence Society. Before proceeding up the hill note the clock above, controlled by rods from a mechanism to be found in the west tower of the church at the other end of the building.

At the top of the Hill, across the road (the junction of East-cheap and Great Tower Street) stands the church of **St. Margaret Pattens (6).** Founded originally in 1067 it was severely damaged in the Great Fire and rebuilt by Wren between 1684 and 1689, the steeple being added in 1703. Its curious affix is said to have originated either in the name of an early benefactor, Patins, or from patterns, a type of clog worn over the ordinary shoe in wet weather, which were made near to the church in Rood Lane. The church, now the Christian Study Centre, has pews at the west end bearing the initials 'CW' said to stand for Christopher Wren, until one remembers that they can also stand for church warden! Beneath the beadle's stall on the left of the altar is a punishment bench, a place to which children were sent for misbehaving in church.

Outside the church, turn right, and walk down **Eastcheap,** but not before noting the very fine Georgian shopfronts on your left just by the church wall. Shortly, on your right, is Philpot Lane. Just a few yards in on your right, look up and find the **two grey mice (7).** The story is told how one day, when the building was being erected in the nineteenth century, a workman brought his customary bread and cheese for his mid-day meal, laying it down on the scaffold where he had been working. Suddenly one of his workmates drew his attention to the meal which was being devoured by two grey mice. He must have been a kindhearted fellow for, so the story goes, he left the creatures to finish his lunch for him, and then asked one of the plasterers to immortalise the story.

Leaving our mice to their cheese we walk up Philpot Lane, cross Fenchurch Street, getting its name from the Foin Church, near an ancient hay-market, and so come to **Lime Street,** which at the close of the eighteenth century was inhabited by many wealthy city merchants. Today there is little or nothing to detain us, and so we walk on to **Leadenhall Market (8),** one of London's chief poultry markets. It stands on the site of the old Leaden Hall, manor house of the Nevill family, which was later purchased for the City of London by Mayor Richard (Dick) Whittington. The market dates from the Middle Ages, although the present building was erected in 1881 to the designs of Sir Horace Jones who, a few years earlier, had also built Smithfield Market. The forum stood here in Roman times and underneath many of the shops are traces of foundations of the great basilica (the courts of law and the market and meeting place of Roman London). Leadenhall Market suffered in the Great Fire but was not wholly destroyed, thanks to a rich merchant who threw money to the crowd so that buildings surrounding it were pulled down to make a break in the way of the flames.

Following through the market and Whittington Avenue on the other side, one comes to Leadenhall Street. Turn left, and in a few yards you will come to an important junction in the city's roadways. Here meet Leadenhall Street, Gracechurch Street and Bishopsgate, the exact spot where roads met in Roman times and where, once, London Stone is said to have been. Look up, across Gracechurch Street and you will see a **blue plaque (9)** indicating that the Standard of Cornhill once stood here.

Cross the road and walk down Cornhill and you will find, on your left, the parish church of **St. Peter-upon-Cornhill (10),** once claimed to have been founded by King Lucius in 179 A.D.— in 1879 they celebrated seventeen hundred years of Christianity on this site! Today the church continues to serve the parish for which it was built and, in addition, acts as the Regimental Church of the Royal Tank Regiment. Destroyed in the Great Fire St. Peter's was rebuilt by Wren in 1680; its rood screen, one of only two Post-Reformation screens, is said to have been the personal work of Wren, because it was in the senior church of the city. One of the building's prized possessions is the keyboard of the organ used by Mendelssohn when he played here in 1840. In addition the church also owns a 'withdrawing table', a Communion Table which was withdrawn from the body of the church after use—thereby showing that it was not an altar of sacrifice for the offering up of the Mass, as in former times.

Back in Cornhill once more, and turning to our left outside the church of St. Peter, another church is soon discovered— **St. Michael's, Cornhill (11)**. This church had a Saxon foundation, and in 1055 was given to the abbots of Evesham, who continued to draw tithes from it until the Reformation in the sixteenth century. The present church is by Wren, but was much altered in the nineteenth century by the late Sir Gilbert Scott. In the churchyard here were buried John Stow's father and grandfather, although there is no longer any trace of their graves. Thomas Gray, the poet, was baptised here, and there are several memorials to the Cowper family who worshipped at St. Michael's.

We have now reached one of the city's most intriguing 'back-doubles'—St. Michael's Alley—leading us to more interesting places behind the busy streets. But first we track down, on our left in St. Michael's Alley, a blue plaque informing us that here was London's first coffee house, The Pasqua Rosee (The Easter Rose). A junction is now reached; on the right is the **George and Vulture Tavern (12)**. Before the Great Fire there were two taverns, one the George, which claimed to be the oldest in the city, having been converted in the twelfth century from an ordinary house into an ale-house, the other called the Lively Vulture. After the fire they were amalgamated. Stories regarding its long and interesting history are innumerable but the one told most often refers to Charles Dickens, discovering the George and Vulture on one of his walking tours of the city and throwing his hat up in the air, overjoyed that he had found another quaint old tavern to put in his books. Thus it was that Mr Pickwick and Sam Weller stayed at the George and Vulture for some little while before departing for Dingley Dell.

Retracing our steps a few yards we turn down Castle Court, finding on our right **Ball Court**, which although it is a dark entry appearing to lead nowhere, in fact takes us down to **Simpson's Chop House (13)**, a perfect 1757 eating house, almost untouched and unspoiled since the day it was first built.

Returning to Castle Court once more, we turn right and, passing under an archway, find ourselves in **Birchin Lane (14)**. The Lane first appears in the records of 1286 and takes its name from a local landowner. This is one of a number of thorough-fares coming under the restriction of the City of London Metropolitan Street Act of 1867. This Act forbids you to drive a vehicle of more than four horses down such a street, nor may you carry down it, by hand, any object longer than 36 feet or wider than 8 feet 6 inches. We, however, unloaded and on

Shank's Pony, need not worry but must look for Change Alley across the road.

Change Alley was previously called Exchange Alley because two of its five openings led into Cornhill and the Royal Exchange. We enter by Birchin Lane and soon find, on our right, another entrance bearing a blue plaque on its corner stating that the Marine Society was founded here. Opposite is yet another plaque, this time in stone, pin-pointing the site of the famous **Garraway's Coffee House (15),** one of the first city merchants to sell tea, at prices ranging from 16 shillings to 50 shillings per pound. Incidentally, next door to Garraway's was Jonathan's Coffee House, the original rendezvous of the stockbrokers and jobbers who were later to form the City of London Stock Exchange. Either exit on your left will bring you to **Lombard Street,** the 'street of the greatest credit in Europe', as a writer once put it, reminding us that here the bankers of Lombardy held forth daily for the purpose of lending money.

Turn right, down Lombard Street, and at its junction with King William Street you will find the church of **St. Mary Woolnoth (16).** The first documented evidence for this church dates from the end of the twelfth century, but the foundation may well be Saxon. In which case it might have received its affix from a Saxon or Danish benefactor; alternatively, there may have been a medieval benefactor with such a name. It survived the Great Fire but in 1717 was demolished and rebuilt by Nicholas Hawksmoor, one of Wren's pupils; there is a distinct influence of Vanbrugh in whose offices Hawksmoor also worked for a time. Edward Lloyd, owner of the coffee-house that was to launch, in the seventeenth century, Lloyd's of London, was buried in the old church. When the Bank Underground Station was built below the church in 1901 there were storms of protests, but today no one seems to notice the novelty of going beneath a place of worship to get into a station. Notice the inscription over one of the station's doorways on the King William Street side of the building which reads 'Lift up your hearts . . .'; one feels inclined to add, 'but mind your heads, the doorway is very low . . .'.

King William Street was constructed between 1831 and 1835, forming part of the road system from the city to south London, via London Bridge. It was considered by some to be one of London's greatest improvements of the nineteenth century. Today, most of the buildings in the street date from the turn of the century and barely merit a second glance. At the far end one finds little Clement's Lane with its Wren church of **St. Clement (17),** Eastcheap, replacing a structure of the thirteenth century destroyed by the Fire. This church is one of the two churches contending to be the St. Clement's referred to in the famous nursery rhyme.

Ignore the complex road junction, cross King William Street and the end of Cannon Street, then turn right with King William Street in the direction of London Bridge until, on the next corner, you come to the **Square Rigger public house (18)**, with its built-in seascapes and screeching seagulls. Across the main road from here is Monument Street and the Monument where, not so long before, we began our search for the first day of the Great Fire of London of 1666.

INDEX

Abbey Bookshop 33
Aldersgate 6
Aldwych 13
All Saints, Chelsea 18
American Club 42
Anne, Queen (statue) 29
Architectural Press 29
Argyll House 17

Ball Court 52
Barber Surgeons' Hall 7
Barton Street 32
Battersea Bridge 19
Baynard's Castle 34
Beaufort Street 20
Bell Yard 15
Berkeley Square 44
Birchin Lane 52
Bishopsgate 51
Black Friar (pub) 39
Blackfriars 33, 38, 39
Blackfriars Bridge 34
Blackfriars Lane 39
Blackfriars Station (BR) 34
Bouverie Street 24
Britten's Court 24
Broad Sanctuary 31
Broadway 29
'Burghers of Calais' 32

Carcy Street 15
Carlyle's House 18
Carter Lane 37
Central Hall 30
Change Alley 53
Charles Street 43
Cheapside 9
Chelsea Town Hall 17

Cheyne Row 18
Child's Bank 21
Church Entry 38-39
Church House 33
City of London Police
   Station 9
Clare Market 9, 13
Clarges Street 40
Clermont Club 44
Clive of India's House 44
Cock (pub) 48
College of Arms 36
Cornhill 51
Crosby Hall 19
Curzon Street 43

Danvers Street 19
Dartmouth House 43
Dean's Court 37
Dean's Yard 33
Duke's House 18

Eastcheap 50
Elsing Priory 8-9

Farm Street 44
Fenchurch Street 51
Fetter Lane 24
Fleet Prison 26
Fleet Street 21
Fore Street 8

Garraway's Coffee House
   53
Gatehouse Prison 30
Geo. Fred. Watts
   Memorial Cloisters 6

George and Vulture 52
George V (statue) 31
Glebe Place 18
Goodes 45
Gough Square 24
Gracechurch Street 51
Great College Street 33
Gresham Street 6
Grosvenor Chapel 45
Grosvenor Square 46

Hoare's Bank 23
Horn Tavern 36-37
Houses of Parliament 3

Immaculate Conception
   Church of 45
Ireland Yard 38

Jewel Tower 32
Johnson, Samuel (statue) 1
Johnson's Court 24
Justice Walk 18

Kennel Club 40
King's Road 17, 20
King William Street 53
Knightrider Street 36

Law Courts 10
Lawrence of Arabia's house
   32
Lawrence Street 18
Leadenhall Market 51
Lime Street 51
Lincoln's Inn 14
Lincoln's Inn Fields 13
Lindsay House 20

Lombard Street 53
London House of St. Edward 33
London School of Economics 13
London Wall 7
Lord North Street 32
Lower Thames Street 50

Magpie Alley 24
Margaret Roper Gardens 19
Mary, Queen of Scots (statue) 25
Mayfair 40
Mermaid Theatre 34
Mice, Two Grey 50
Middlesex Guildhall 31
Middle Temple 22
Mitre Court (Fleet St.) 24
Mitre Court (Wood St.) 9
Mitre Tavern 23
Monmouth House 18
Monument 48
More, Sir Thomas (statue) 15, 19

Naval and Military Club 42
Newcastle House 14
New Hall 15
Noble Street 7

Old Church Street 18
Old Curiosity Shop 13
Old Hall 15

Palmerston, Lord (birthplace) 30
Pankhurst, Mrs (statue) 32
Parish boundary stones 15
Pasqua Rosee 52
Paultons Square 20
Pepys, Samuel (birthplace) 25

Petty France 29
Philpot Lane 50
Piccadilly 40
Playhouse Yard 38
Poppins Court 26
Prince Henry's Room 22
Pudding Lane 48
Purdey's 46

Queen Anne's Gate 29
Queen Street, Mayfair 43
Queen Victoria Street 36

Roman boundary stone 31
Roosevelt, Franklin (statue) 46
Royal College of Surgeons 14
Royal Courts of Justice 10
Running Footman 44

St. Alban's tower 9
St. Andrew-by-the-Wardrobe 38
St. Anne and St. Agnes 7
St. Ann's, Blackfriars 38
St. Benet's 36
St. Botolph's, Aldersgate 5
St. Bride's, Fleet St. 25
St. Clement Danes 12
St. Clement Eastcheap 53
St. Dunstan's-in-the-West 22
St. Giles, Cripplegate 7
St. James's Park Station 27
St. John the Evangelist, Westminster 32
St. Margaret Pattens 50
St. Margaret's Street 31
St. Margaret's, Westminster 31
St. Martin le Grand 5

St. Mary at Hill 50
St. Mary Woolnoth 53
St. Michael's, Cornhill 52
St. Paul's Choir School 37
St. Paul's Deanery 37
St. Peter's, West Chepe 9
St. Peter-upon-Cornhill 51
Salisbury Court 25
Salisbury Square 25
Sardinia Street 13
Sergeant's Inn 24
Seven Stars 15
Shepherd Market 42
Ship Tavern 14
Simpson's Chop House 52
Six Bells 17
Smith Square 32
Soane's Museum 14
Society of Apothecaries 39
South Audley Street 45
Square Rigger 54

Temple Bar 15, 21
Tothill Street 30
Tyburn River 42

United States Embassy 46
Upper Cheyne Row 18
Upper Thames Street 34

Wall, City 5, 7, 8,
Wallace, Edgar (plaque) 26
Wardrobe Place 37
Watermen's Hall 50
Westminster Abbey 27
Westminster School 33
Whitehorse Street 42
Wood Street 9

Ye Olde Cheshire Cheese 24

Some titles available in the 'Discovering' series

Antique Maps
Archaeology in Denmark
Archaeology in England and Wales
Avon
Backgammon
Banknotes
Battlefields of Scotland
Beekeeping
Bells and Bellringing
Bird Watching
Brasses and Brassrubbing
British Cavalry Regiments
British Ponies
Burns Country
Cambridgeshire
Canals
Carts and Wagons
Castle Combe
Castles in England and Wales
Cathedrals
Chapels
Cheshire
Chess
Christmas Customs
Churches
Church Architecture
Corn Dollies
Edged Weapons
English Folk Dance
English Furniture
English Literary Associations
Essex
Famous Battles: Marlborough's Campaigns
Famous Battles: Peninsular War
Folklore and Customs of Love and Marriage
Folklore of Plants
French and German Military Uniforms
Garden Insects
Gardening for the Handicapped
Hallmarks on English Silver
Hampshire
Herbs
Highwaymen
Hill Figures
Horse Brasses
Horse Drawn Carriages
Horse Drawn Commercial Vehicles
Industrial Archaeology
Kent
Kings and Queens
Lakeland
Leicestershire and Rutland
Lincolnshire
London for Children

London Street Names
London Villages
Lost Canals
Lost Railways
Magic Charms and Talismans
Mah-jong
Mechanical Music
Military Traditions
Model Soldiers
Mottoes
Norfolk
Northamptonshire
Northumbria
Off-beat Walks in London
Oil Lamps
Old Aeroplanes
Old Board Games
Old Motor Cycles
Pantomime
Period Gardens
Place Names
Quantocks
Regional Archaeology series:
    North-Eastern
    North-Western
    South-Eastern
    South-Western
    Wales
The Ridgeway
Salop
Schools
South Yorkshire
Space
Staffordshire
Stately Homes
Statues in Cent. & N. Eng.
Statues in S. England
Suffolk
Surnames
Sussex
Thames and Chilterns
Theatre Ephemera
Topiary
Towns
Walks in the Cotswolds
Walks in Hertfordshire
Walks in the New Forest
Walks in Wessex Towns
Walks in West Sussex
Watermills
Westward Stage
Windmills
Your Family Tree

*From your bookseller or from Shire Publications Ltd.,
Cromwell House, Church Street, Princes Risborough,
Aylesbury, Bucks., U.K.*